Effective Threat Intelligence

Building and Running an Intel Team for Your Organization

James Dietle

Printed in the United States of America

First Printing, 2016

ISBN 13: 978-1533314550
ISBN: 1533314551
Library of Congress Control Number: 2016909904
CreateSpace Independent Pub. Platform, North Charleston, SC

Author can be contacted through www.MindTrinket.com.

Special discounts are available on quantity purchases by corporations, associations, and others. For details, contact the author at jdietle@mindtrinket.com

To little Addy, thanks for only slightly gnawing on my computer.

Table of Contents

1

Introduction to Threat Intelligence

Cyberthreat intelligence is being treated as a new business essential that can only be done by a select few at great cost. This book will help you better understand the concept of threat intelligence and break it into easy steps to improve your company, no matter the size. Additionally, I will explore and dispel some of the myths of threat intelligence and help you understand what initiatives you should pursue or research in order to make your company information technology (IT) safer for your employees and your clients.

Remember *Starship Troopers*? It was a campy sci-fi movie where men and bugs battled on distant alien worlds with silly action scenes. Everybody followed around the grunt, Johnny Rico, glamorizing the importance of being the hero on the field. However, toward the end of the movie, we learn how the grunt work, which is often grueling and never glamorous, is also useless if improperly applied. Throughout the film, protagonists wage interstellar campaigns to gain intelligence by stealing a "Brain Bug."

The entire movie focuses on a group trying to gain better intelligence during a war.

Like in the movie, there seems to be a push to treat information security as a kind of "war." We have our "grunts" in the trenches slogging over digital fields, doing long hours of work unappreciated by most and misunderstood by all.

The truth is everyone already operates some kind of threat-intelligence model. Although some groups are doing this more formally than others, your boss, your teammates, and you are ready to take better advantage of what you already know. Threat intelligence is simply a refining of the same principles we have grown up with and cut our teeth on in the IT field. With the higher number of large-scale incidents, like those seen at Anthem and Sony, employees outside of IT have started to realize fears that have kept nerds up late at night.

However, all hope is not lost. While there are many new faces, threats, groups, and bad guys, understanding your advisory is always valuable. While I don't claim to have the perfect answers, I do believe many groups are closer than they thought.

I intend this book to be less of an instruction manual and involve a more Socratic method in helping you identify potential gaps in your own or your company's knowledge.

What Is Threat Intelligence?

Threat intelligence is a relatively new buzzword, but the use of intelligence, or the problem of understanding information, has been around for a long time. Applying threat intelligence (intel) to IT security has become a booming business, with companies and individuals setting up businesses to commoditize it, package it, ship it, and sell it. Some groups are using the term *intelligence* as a prefix for their newest products, while others list *intelligence* among various other adjectives on product sheets.

From tangibles to intangibles, everyone has a different idea of what intelligence is. What I find fascinating is how the definition for intelligence changes even among some of the most sophisticated organizations.

In a bold attempt to simplify matters, I propose that the best way to look at intelligence is with the following definition:

Intelligence is information that is used to make a decision.

A quick Google search will show similar definitions: "The ability to acquire and *apply* knowledge and skills," and "The collection of *information of* military or political *value*." If there is no value added, intelligence is simply information. If it is not used, nobody cares. I feel, given this perspective, we can easily posit that an excess of information will lead to worse intelligence, as it becomes harder to act upon. Therefore, the essential point is that for information to be intelligence, it needs to be used and add value.

Adversaries and threat actors are interchangeable terms that describe a person or group wishing to misuse a company's assets to further personal motivations.

This can be in the form of stealing customer credit-card numbers, stealing funds, or destroying equipment. This book helps describe how gathering more information about adversaries can help stop them.

Taking this to the next logical step:

***Threat* intelligence is *information about* adversaries that is used to make a decision.**

It is important to emphasize that the major effort we are hoping to achieve with threat intelligence is understanding what the adversaries are thinking, feeling, and doing, so we may counter their attacks as easily as possible.

Consideration of the corporate infrastructure, physical security reports, patching management, and vulnerabilities all help shape a security profile. All the attributes have a critical role in the security structure of the company. Nonetheless, these examples are not of adversaries but rather of self-reflection. While essential to information security, and certainly meriting a Sun Tzu quote, this is not threat intelligence.

Threat intelligence as described in this book will focus us outward and concentrates on the attacks and intentions of adversaries. Adversaries rarely telegraph their moves, aren't open to talk with you, and will leave few to no clues. Just like a crime scene in real life, it is challenging. As I discuss threat intelligence, I will always focus on the adversaries and hopefully be ahead of their actions.

I Think You Need More Intelligence

There is this problem where simply stating a need for "intelligence" seems a little strange. Imagine your boss going out and saying, "You know what? We need more intelligence in this organization." Doesn't this imply you are dumb? That you are in some way, shape, or form "unintelligent"?

Yet this seems to be a popular narrative as vendors try to sell something that is extremely complex in a single word.

Buying intelligence like a nice little package is a fantasy. It doesn't exist.

Information is bought and sold. However, a person makes it into intelligence. Only you and your employees can turn information into intelligence, because only you can make decisions on how to act on the information that you purchase.

Why Is Intelligence Important Anyway?

Imagine knowing your opponent's next move in chess.

- Why is that important?
- How valuable would that be?
- How would you feel if your opponent could have this information?
- Do you feel as if you have an unfair advantage?

Claude Shannon is famous for discussing information theory, a discipline that has been around for longer than we imagine. Famously, he worked on programming computers to play chess and getting them to "think" like a human.

Successful chess players are able to anticipate their opponent's moves in advance. The best chess players in the world are able to predict what their opponents are going to do many moves in advance. By studying your opponent, you can make better tactical decisions. Similarly, if you know your digital opponents, their motivations, tactics, and desires, you will be able to better defend and counter their attacks.

When you know an adversary is going to conduct a Distributed Denial of Service (DDoS) attack at 9:00 a.m. on Tuesday, what should you do? When you can estimate the size of the DDoS, know how they are targeting your industry, and determine that your system is robust enough to withstand previously observed attacks, you can be confident the company is prepared if they come your way. More importantly, you can bring this information to other people in the organization to let them know it is handled.

This level of thinking and planning is certainly much more difficult in real life than in chess. Chess is extremely restricted in movement. In the real world, there are more moves and more players in the game. However, looking at basic information theory and observing the value of intelligence with a simpler model is a great experience for allowing people to initially dive into information theory and realize how most people create threat intelligence every day.

Teasing Out Patterns from Models

Models help ensure that important information is being properly recognized and allow for patterns to emerge. Through the use of models, organizations can understand many different aspects throughout their organizations and the potential threats to them.

Understanding these aspects is a difficult task, and many organizations struggle to really define their needs for many information sources, including information used to make decisions. When determining what information a company should use for their basis of information, I suggest creating a model.

Even a crude model can provide valuable insight. Models are important because they attempt to answer how something will be accomplished on a small scale. Just as chess is a simplistic model for ancient battle, many other models simplify complex, real-world events. Risk in today's business world can also be modeled to help understand how information will assist various aspects of the business. The military is famous for conducting war games, which are models of real-world problems broken down into a simpler simulation.

Models are a way we can test what information will help lead us to a better decision, or what intelligence might change our game plan. By understanding what you wish you knew, you have identified what intelligence the organization should be collecting and can even prioritize which information should be collected.

A helpful model to consider is how the CDC treats virus outbreaks. Hunting down an elusive virus is a difficult task that relies on many factors. Simulations of disease spread share some similar aspects as threat actors. The smallpox simulation Dark Winter helps the CDC understand potential hosts, environmental factors, and even population density. Thousands of hosts are simulated, and human behavior is added as a component. This model helps the CDC understand how a virus is expected to travel; it allows them a certain amount of intelligence to be used in selecting vaccines and changing public policy. However, it also shows what intelligence they might be missing and what they would need to do to make better decisions.

This model is fascinating because it mirrors many of the same problems a security professional would see. People not washing hands may transmit a virus much in the same way as people falling victim to a phishing attack after not observing proper e-mail hygiene.

If we take these lessons from other organizations in different specialties such as the CDC and the military have done, we aren't starting an intelligence program from scratch. We can observe several things on the micro scale, such as these:

- Malware behavior
- Network traffic logs
- Threats
- Indicators of compromise
- Strange host behavior

Proper models can help define the information to be collected to produce solid intelligence about threats to your network. Once this is established, the company can use the information, understand the threat, and make decisions on how to protect your company from it.

I suggest that as you try to produce your own model for your company, you play around with it to determine what the team thinks is important. It doesn't have to be perfect (it's important to identify the flaws of a model), and it lets you discover what is important in your environment. While specific indicators are discussed later, observation from a simplistic model of information in the network and through host evaluation can lead to threat intelligence that we can leverage in our environments.

Collecting the Raw Information

With everyone attempting to sell "threat intelligence," there should be some discussion about how it is collected. Historically, intelligence collection is viewed as the monstrously big antennas acting as gigantic ears pulling in information from the across the world. Interconnected with custom-designed-and-built hardware, these behemoths were operated by numerous people as full-time jobs. Gathering intelligence on this scale was cost prohibitive, and only governments were able to acquire enough technology, gear, and, most importantly, trained employees to operate these machines. It was an extremely expensive and an exceedingly complex process. This foundation created a mind-set in which most people believe that threat intelligence is a large and difficult undertaking.

Today is a new age for intelligence. Information is pulled, scraped, gathered, sold, and stolen by all kinds of people in all kinds of venues. The ability to gather information is no longer too expensive for individuals and is frankly awe-inspiring. While the past was marred by the complexity of gathering data and hindered by its scarcity, today there is such a massive glut of data that we are hindered by the ability to filter and process it.

Information that can be used in a technical environment may come from many sources. Technical information can be pulled from network logs and pieces of the malware captured. Threats from hacktivists or blackmailers can be shared. Reports compiling the majority of these thoughts can be sent to executives to make strategic decisions. There are also nontechnical areas in which threat intelligence can be discovered. Social media is now rife with information regarding people, technologies, and even manuals on how hardware works. All of this information can be made into intelligence, and it can all be used to make a decision. The question is how.

Where Do You Get It?

Since we know that threat intelligence is a good thing to create, compile, and use, we need to know the best places to go in order to get it, and every source has its advantages and disadvantages.

Open Source

Open-source intelligence is commonly referred to as OSINT in military circles. OSINT is information someone can find or discover easily without specific accesses or knowledge. Traditionally, this was gathered through newspapers or word of mouth or by simply reading technical manuals for products. However, new digital formats have expanded this greatly.

As newspapers were once a common place to gather OSINT, digital media has expanded the newspapers' reach considerably. Security-breach information has become a more popular mainstream topic. Great information can be drawn from these reports and can be used to better understand the adversary's intentions, techniques, or motivations. As we continue to read these bits and pieces of information, a good intelligence analyst will be able to notice trends occurring in his or her sphere of influence.

For example, currently the Anthem and Premera breaches contain similar indicators shared by major media outlets. Researchers, engineers, and politicians noticed that the threat behind these breaches focused on medical records. Now companies that have medical records should understand that not only are these documents important to protect, but also groups are actively looking for these files to steal. Several articles even give out indicators an investigator could use to protect them against this type of threat.

The best part about newspapers is they are normally free or at least extremely cheap. Unfortunately, some of the information can be stale, time-consuming to sort through, and in some cases wrong. Actionable information is out there (for free), and just like the sleuths from the movies, you can learn quite a bit from newspapers.

RSS Feeds

RSS feeds can be a tool to ensure that your group receives immediate updates from your favorite information sources. Sharing many of the same characteristics as newspapers, RSS feeds can offer a near-endless supply of information.

The biggest problem with RSS feeds is the humongous amount of data pushed to your organization. The feeds can bury your team alive with information that might be redundant, dated, or wrong. However, they are cheap and normally one of the first ways a company can start building a fledgling threat-intelligence program.

Proprietary Feeds

Like normal RSS feeds, proprietary feeds can come in a variety of methods, including text files, HTML files, and various APIs. The only constant is these are not shared with everyone. There is either a special membership or a special fee for receiving the feeds.

The look and feel of proprietary feeds can vary greatly, from straight HTML files of IPs and MD5s to sweeping narratives and analyses about the most dangerous digital hooligans. Unlike open-source information, proprietary information relies on exclusivity and a limited audience to help protect criminals from changing their indicators.

Proprietary feeds can be highly beneficial if they are correctly fitted to your organization. Two important considerations when choosing to purchase proprietary feeds are how the information can be used and whether they are meeting the goals for your threat-intelligence program. If they are not, or if you later find they are not being as effective as you would like, cut them.

Social Media

Social media has exploded with discussion about exploits, vulnerabilities, and hacks of the day. Selling yourself, your company, or your ideal is important to grow recognition and street cred. From hacktivists to established security firms, everyone is out there trying to look and sound important.

Luckily, this information is great for the analyst. Hacktivists are keen on trying to gain notoriety by sharing their latest exploits and conquests. Someone following various feeds or sites might notice emerging trends. The best example is the "Anonymous" movement. Often depicted as kids with foul senses of humor, Anonymous users have had some successes when trying to take down websites with DDoS and open-source tools that are readily available on the web. Fortunately, the decentralized nature of hacktivists compels them to use open communication channels.

Large security companies also like to boast about their latest findings. Since "Heartbleed" there has been a movement to brand threat actors, vulnerabilities, and exploits. When Qualys released the "Ghost" exploit, they didn't stop at a single social-media site. They released information on LinkedIn, Twitter, Facebook, and a custom website. All of these free resources provided by companies on social media can help shortcut the discovery process of emerging tools or techniques.

Following many social-media sites can allow analysts to see some very basic trending. If the content shown to them is massive and discusses a similar problem, it is probably something they should at least look into.

Twitter

While several forms of social media exist, one of the popular and interesting ones is Twitter. The constraint of only 140 characters forces an otherwise long and winding discussion to take place rapidly. This forces a short synopsis that allows the analyst to figure out what is going on without devoting too much time to it. In the event that an analyst needs more information, tweets often link information articles related to the topic. This creates a "too long; didn't read" message to gauge interest, and a direct link if you happen to be interested.

I recommend following security companies and prominent researchers. It is simple and effective at pulling in data trending across the world. After all, it is their job to stay on top of security, so when they compete to get detailed information out quickly, you can see it blowing up on your Twitter account.

A rudimentary way to gauge the value of Twitter tweets is to consider the retweets and likes. Typically, more accurate and helpful tweets are more popular. If you notice popularity among some tweets, they may have better information about a certain threat. This is also true if other security researchers are sharing it.

Like most feeds, Twitter feeds need to be cultivated over time. If you find that people are cluttering up your account with no useful information, unfollow them. Twitter will also recommend new accounts to follow, which can be helpful to discover what new feeds to read or consider.

Setting up a Twitter account is free and easy. Even if you have never had a Twitter account and will just be lurking, I recommend setting up a free account and following some of the bigger names. Look at feeds and see if that type of information is something you would be interested in.

Researcher Sites

There are several great sites produced by researchers showing their work and analysis of malware they encounter. Deconstructing attack methods and tactics is difficult work, and researchers providing it for free are heroes. These sites often provide the analysis but also may provide samples picked up from the wild.

Extensive details from malware are passed quickly to the reader. Often these sites provide step-by-step instructions on how the malware was deconstructed. This information can be passed along to the responders who can move straight to the interesting bits for your company.

The researchers' sites are great because they are often free, provide great visuals, and help you save time. They also can show what is happening to your peers with actionable information.

YouTube

YouTube offers some of the same benefits of Twitter. The ne'er-do-wells and the cyberpaladins have been using this format to explain their latest products, procedures, proof of concepts, and proof of damage. Videos are a fantastic medium because they are easy to set up and make it easy to step through explicit descriptions of what is happening.

From my own experience, I have learned a great deal about exploits from various YouTube videos. Security researchers are quick to try to reproduce the latest vulnerabilities and show exactly how they work. The company Rapid 7 does a great job with this by producing useful examples and whiteboard exercises demonstrating how these new named exploits work and how to use them with metasploit. These examples are invaluable. They allow you to really take a look at the exploit and decide if the threat is something important to your environment. They also allow you to recreate the exploit in a test environment so you can gauge the impact on the production environment.

Additionally, exploits and propaganda placed on the web help explain targeting and reasons for the targeting. With the recent rise in political hacktivism, we have seen more threats of low-level attacks and threats being shown on the web. ISIS sympathizers have been using quick, easy, and dirty exploits to help spread their message. To garner support, that information is posted online with their intent and their motives.

YouTube can also explain extremely complex issues in a visually appealing manner to executives. A win-win example of this is the Dark Hotel threat actor that Kaspersky Labs released information about. The video is perfect; it has visual appeal, accurately displays the threat actor, and is, most importantly, short. Instead of writing a large report, simply attach the video for executives, bypass the extra fluff, and get onto the solution. The video is often framed more like a company advertisement than a report; you should feel no problems with sending it to your executives. I'm sure the company appreciates the additional exposure.

The most difficult problem with YouTube videos is that they are hard to search quickly, and scraping the information is cumbersome. Videos can range from three minutes to three hours long. Ads included in the YouTube experience also slow you down from getting content. This differs greatly from text-based options available to search for text on websites, blogs, and Twitter feeds with various scrapers. I would recommend sticking to alternative feeds and using YouTube to supplement your knowledge or as a tool to explain an exploit or threat actor.

Podcasts

Similar to YouTube videos, podcasts have become popular for researchers and companies alike. The reduced production requirements allow for a quicker turnaround, which in turn allows for more recent information and a higher volume. Additionally, creating a small, mobile studio can be affordable and easy. These factors have all combined to allow companies and researchers a quick way to build interesting podcasts.

Security podcasts can bring together more people and experts to present on a topic. Participants do not have to board a plane or travel in order to get to the recording studio. Instead they just need to dial up on Skype or call in with their phone. This creates environments where many experts can discuss a certain aspect of security. I find this particularly helpful because each participant can present a different viewpoint on the topic.

To save time, I tend to watch them on double speed—a trick I learned from my cousin during his time at medical school. If something piques my interest, I simply go back and play the audio at normal speed.

Special Sites

Some unique websites include pastebins and file-sharing services, which allow users to anonymously post information and upload data. These sites are favorites since the data, instructions, dumps, and tools can be easily shared to other groups with little to no attribution. In some cases they are even used as a source for coordination among different groups.

However, these sites are difficult to find, are unreliable, and can be temporal. The information is normally unverified, which requires time to check and ensure that it is legitimate. I have seen this occur several times when old data are posted and reused for notoriety or are wrongly attributed. Other times I have seen users attempt to lure readers into running malicious code. If the data dump is either output from a program or designed to be machine readable, an added layer of complexity must be overcome. In these scenarios, the data presented can be very raw and will need additional diligence to be properly checked.

All these concerns can help muddle the value of the information being provided by researching dumps. While the information they provide can vary greatly, these difficulties can make researching a large amount of dumps from special sites too time-consuming to justify.

Deep Web

Researching intelligence through the deep web is fascinating. Typically the deep web is hidden through the use of the Tor network where nobody can be trusted, information is spotty, and everyone is trying to infect each other. The deep web can accurately be described as a black market behind the normal Internet. As the selling of personal data dumps, credit-card numbers, and exploits have become increasingly businesslike, the deep web can help explain which companies might have recently been breached, what threat actors might have stolen, and what they are looking for next.

Data dumps of credit cards and personal information are fairly common in these underground marketplaces. Criminals are selling data such as personal information and credit-card numbers for profit. Criminals walk a fine line between wanting to sell unique information and not wanting to draw attention to it. As with all information, the value in stolen credit-card information is the ability to monetize it. If the pattern is discovered, such as all these stolen credit cards recently made purchases from the same store, actions could be taken to prevent the other cards in that dump from being used.

As defenders, we want to discover this pattern so we can limit the victims as quickly as we can. In doing so, we prevent criminals from further monetizing the data breach. Therefore, criminals attempt to sell data dumps immediately and completely, which might be the first indication a company was compromised.

Advertisements for new exploits and botnets being sold can give analysts an idea of what will soon be used to target their network. For example, if you know a CVE-20XX-XXXX exploit is being sold, it would be prudent to update your services to protect against the vulnerability.

There are several risks with looking into these sites on the deep web. Dangers of infection, tracking of your movement by the site owners, other illegal activities, and false claims all make investigations into the deep web tricky. If you do decide to have a program investigating the sites, I suggest you have some strong defenses (using a VM or Tor network, for example) in place to prevent these dangers.

Many security researchers are already following these sites and criminals on the deep web. It is so prevalent that I feel much of the information appears on public sites quickly. I think that the possible dangers outweigh the benefit of having an intelligence program investigate these options.

Format

Intelligence feeds can come in many formats. The most common is not being formatted at all. Open-source information can come in as many varied formats as you can imagine. The format varies widely from PDF briefings to ad-laced news stories. Receiving information this way is not optimal, because it is not easy to automate and requires an analyst to strip out the important bits and pieces to put into devices or to inform stakeholders.

Files like text files, Excel spreadsheets, and zip files are also popular. These are a bit nicer because they do not have to have user interaction. Instead, they start to offer the possibility of automating intelligence into devices. Files of just IPs, MD5s, or URLs can be dropped into places to read the indicators into the environment.

MITRE is a nonprofit organization that conducts research for the US government. They have been extremely useful in creating standards for sharing information for threat communities. In particular, they are well-known for their classification of vulnerabilities with the CVE system. MITRE has been developing three similar tools for threat intelligence.

TAXII is designed to quickly allow information to be shared among multiple groups in an automated fashion. By stripping away identifying information, TAXII can move data concerning threat actors back and forth without denoting that the target was attacked. By pushing all types of information in one format, the possibility of having machines convey indicators goes up. The hope is to automatically integrate threat information into processes and ensure that the delay before implementation is as short as possible. TAXII comes in a variety of models to share information with varying degrees of ability to push and pull data.

STIX is often used in terms of TAXII and is the common language, techniques, and terminology to group and structure threat intelligence in a standardized manner. This makes it easier to share data among various partners.

Like STIX, CybOX is not truly a field. It is a method to place various indicators into a common language for representing observables. These can be either dynamic observables, like a memory state, or something more specific, like an MD5 hash. The difficulty with using something like CybOX is that some pieces of information do not easily fit into their standards. While IPs, MD5s, and other observables are readily placed into a machine-readable language, more esoteric observables are difficult.

I would recommend as a threat analyst that you understand the type of information that is going on in these methods, but don't limit yourself to it. These open-source methods are in their infancy and still not widely adopted by the industry.

The question is if the information would be used in the environment. If, for example, the largest threats to your organization are illegal manipulation of your processes and creation of false accounts, the STIX, CybOX, and TAXII framework might not be the best fit. These threats are not well defined in the framework and therefore might not lend good threat intelligence. Therefore, you will need to determine a different way to quantify and share these threats.

One fear about the use of automated feeds is the possibility of intelligence being incorrect. I have heard analysts complain about benign indicators being included in threat feeds that would disrupt the environment.

Don't Consume Threat Intelligence Like a Goldfish

The world is full of information for you and your team to gather. Feel free to pick and choose from the sources that make sense to your company, time frame, budget, and experience. The important part is not getting overloaded. If you consume everything you come across, you're bound to make the program simply explode. If the team is spending hours looking through Twitter feeds, and none of the information makes the transition to intelligence for your company, it is time to move on. Surely, you can revisit it later when you have more resources or better technical controls, or when the source provides more actionable information.

Although I have given you many different options to gather information, there are still plenty more floating around. If you find something that works well for your company, please let me know! I will be happy to explore it with you.

Methods of Distribution for Threat-Related Information

Once information is gathered, it can be shared with other groups in several ways.

Internal Distribution

Distributing threat information internally is the easiest method to take information discovered and process it into intelligence. Informal discussion is extremely common, even among nontechnical employees, who may discuss a strange e-mail they just received. At its very core, sharing information among internal teams is the best way to help transition information into threat intelligence.

Unfortunately, only sharing threat intelligence internally is overlooking some major avenues for collaboration among not only internal partners but also other outside groups. To solve this, there are many proponents wishing to push intel out to a much wider audience to piece together the larger threat puzzles.

Selling for Profit

A popular option for security vendors is to sell threat-related information for profit. Investigations of IT incidents are expensive and time-consuming processes, but they produce indicators of threat behavior that can be useful to other companies. Selling the information can contribute to a wider investigation among companies and provide the vendor a small profit for their efforts.

Concerns regarding sharing of incident data are similar to those of internal sharing and require attributing data to be removed from the feeds. Once properly evaluated, sanitized findings can be shared with other companies to protect them against similar threats. For some companies, this sanitized information might be one of the only methods through which they receive threat intelligence.

This distribution method is helpful especially when you get a full account of the information provided. It can be compared with other information seen in other sources and correlated by analysts internal to your organization. This allows your team to properly evaluate and prioritize threats seen in other organizations.

Proprietary Information

Certain vendors distribute threat intelligence by sending information directly to threat-detection software, security information and event managers (SIEMs), and endpoint software. In these models, indicators are uploaded into the corresponding software and hardware to help protect the network. This can be frustrating to security teams when generated alerts have little to no information explaining what caused the alert. This lack of context can be problematic when there is greater difficulty in distinguishing between legitimate and improper detection by the software. Also, feedback will almost always be longer if it is going to an outside party than if it is responded to on-site.

While proprietary feeds create a lack of transparency, they can still be effective for smaller teams and often are included in the licensing of many security products.

Government Threat Sharing

In 2015 President Obama stated the intention to create a cyberthreat intelligence agency. While this is a strong step in the right direction, government sharing is typically difficult and slow. Ask yourself, how well do they share information within their own circles, let alone with civilian counterparts?

However, government feeds can still be a valuable tool in protecting companies from a digital threat. Threat-sharing communities such as InfraGard and US-Cert are examples of US agencies that have been created to share intelligence to curb the threat. Both these examples are free sources of information showing the threats other companies are seeing.

Alternatively, the information and analysis can be provided openly across the world. Several user groups and web forums make use of this technique to share their discoveries with the world.

Sharing Too Far

While more people are advocating for increased transparency, there are still reasons for both a company and a threat-intelligence program to keep information close. Any information that may impact any business dealings, preempt the company's public disclosure of an incident, harm customers, or cause legal complications should be carefully shared after it has been reviewed. Improperly vetted information can lead to loss of revenue, theft of intellectual property, and perhaps lawsuits.

Therefore, it is important to check information before sharing. However, selectively reviewing information to be shared or sanitizing information can be costly, which is why many companies have traditionally preferred to keep information and intelligence internal.

An interesting juxtaposition happens when you share intelligence. The further you spread intelligence, the less useful it can end up being. The famous military saying, "The enemy has a vote," applies, meaning they can change their approach, methods, and tactics, especially if they know you are expecting them.

Let's pretend you discover that a house robber is planning on targeting someone in the neighborhood at 1:00 p.m. If you share the information too widely, the robber will find out that his plans were leaked! The robber might still rob the neighborhood, just at a different time. However, if you limit the information too strictly, your neighbors will not be protected.

The Cardinal Rule of Threat Intelligence

The number-one rule for threat intel is this:

Do not get buried!

As we get excited about building a threat-intelligence program, there are some notes of caution. There is one universal truth in intelligence, and this principle is on par with the universal truths of death and taxes.

There is always more information to gather, and you cannot read it all.

- Do not fall into the trap of trying to read all of it.
- Do not make the mistake of trying to get all of it.
- Do not make the mistake of trying to input all of it. If you are even coming close, you are going to burn out and fail miserably.
- The fastest way to process a piece of information is to ignore it. If you won't or can't do something with it, ignore it.

How much threat intelligence do you need? Just enough to make a decision is the correct, albeit simplistic, answer.

One caveat: make sure you are observing your model and set in time to do so. If you are wrong, and your assumptions are going in a different direction, you need to spend time to correct it.

What Is Good Threat Intel?

SQL Slammer is famous for infecting over eighty thousand computers in under ten minutes. An ingenious buffer overflow, it attacked port 1434 of random IP addresses to get around the world quickly. This unique virus also created an excellent sample of threat intelligence. Michael Bacarella sent out the message "MS SQL WORM IS DESTROYING INTERNET BLOCK PORT 1434!" on seclists.org.

I like the SQL Slammer example because the information provided by Bacarella is actionable, certain, and timely. He told people which port to block, included no extraneous information, and stated that the attack was ongoing. Therefore, I suggest that the definition of good intelligence is how closely it mirrors the SQL Slammer response. A good threat-intelligence response should strive to meet the three standards outlined as follows.

Actionable: Intelligence Can Be Acted Upon

The most important aspect of good intelligence is how the security team is able to implement the information. Information with no practical use to researchers might be interesting but is far from useful. Luckily, most intelligence feeds provide information an analyst can easily use.

For example, one method of describing software behavior is YARA rules. While YARA rules can look at many different types of behavior, they are often used to describe malware behavior seen on host computers or servers. Some threat-intelligence feeds include YARA rules to help companies detect malware on their computers.

Unfortunately, not all devices are able to implement YARA rules.

If devices you are protecting do not use YARA rules, these feeds will not be beneficial to your group. Therefore, intelligence in the form of YARA rules might not be actionable in your environment. This is not to say they are not useful elsewhere, just not for your environment at this time.

Information that is not actionable can be dangerous. It can lure good employees away from producing more meaningful intelligence. Worse yet, very hard-to-action information can create a large amount of work under the guise of good intentions. Employees can be sucked through rabbit holes in which they spend hours for little benefit to the organization. While the degree of actionability of information seems obvious, ensuring that the information produces good and actionable results is sometimes overlooked.

Since an intelligence feed may provide a great many data points, it might be difficult to implement all of them into your environment. Some examples are these:

- Files might need to be manually updated.
- Information could be provided in a poor format.
- Information might be useful only in a small part of the infrastructure.

It's worth taking a good, hard look to determine if you want to dedicate the number of work hours required to implement all the information you are collecting.

I discuss actionability first because it is the only attribute that can be determined before events happen in the environment. To assess both certainty and timeliness, events will need to have already happened.

Certainty: Likeliness and Impact of It Happening

Making fun of weather reporters is a time-honored tradition, and weather reports are a type of intelligence everyone can relate to. Weather predictions have gotten remarkably better over the past years with the help of advanced computer modeling, and, yet, weather reporters continue to foster this idea of "weather guessers." For as much time and effort as we are spending to make predictions, it is better if we do not lump ourselves into this category of intelligence "guessers."

Although weather reporters can't really catch a break, intelligence specialists in other fields need to keep a similar thought of caution. Intelligence can offer suggestions on how threats will materialize, and I urge you to consider a kind of probabilistic forecast to go along with your intelligence dissemination.

In his book *The Signal and the Noise*, Nate Silver explains certainty and the weather-reporter problem. People give weather reporters a hard time precisely because weather intelligence is used to make everyday decisions. Sometimes people decide to cancel a picnic if poor weather is forecasted. If they then see a perfectly sunny day, they aren't pleased that they canceled. This is similar to how managers, users, and executives make decisions considering threat intelligence. When executives spend thousands of dollars on a firewall upgrade that was not needed, they are not pleased.

We can measure a certainty rating in hindsight. By reviewing threat intelligence, we can determine what was useful in our environment. If a feed gave us IPs to block, we could determine the number of these that we had seen in our environment that were malicious traffic. We could use the resulting number as a certainty rating to evaluate the certainty of the feed.

Timeliness: When You Should Expect It to Happen

Timing matters. If the intelligence is constantly provided late and after an incident, it is not beneficial. More importantly, longer lead times allow defenders to proactively defend the network and get out ahead of the threat. Like putting up sandbags for a flood or stockpiling water for a hurricane, the longer you have, the more prepared you can be. The longer timeline is especially important if preparing defenses is more time intensive, such as redesigning network architecture or applications.

It is extremely difficult to build effective defenses cheaply, effectively, and quickly without some form of threat intelligence. Instead of scrambling for new information during a major event, you can prepare for a crisis. Companies can put in additional mitigations or remove vulnerable data from the system. Threat intelligence is the only way to actively achieve this.

The timeliness of information is also easy to gauge and understand. You can just measure the time from when an event occurred to when information pointing to the threat was provided. That difference between the times should be as large as possible. If other feeds are providing good information sooner, they will be more valuable to the organization.

Timely, Certain, and Actionable Intelligence

By combining the actionability, certainty, and timeliness of threat intelligence, we are beginning to build a vocabulary of defining and separating the "good" from the "bad." This helps us determine which bits of information we should take with us and which actions we should prioritize for the next year, month, and even hour. It also allows us to correct the cost of threat intelligence by dropping feeds that are not providing actionable, certain, and timely data. We can then replace them with something that meets these requirements.

The Uncertainty of Threat Intelligence

Unfortunately, despite all my love for chess, it does not make a good model for defending a network. Beyond the black-and-white board, threat intelligence has uncertainty from countless possibilities transcending the restraints and constraints of chess. This is the difficulty of trying to predict how threat actors may move and act. Some threat actors are exploring a national agenda, and some of the same information and intelligence techniques used in foreign policy are readily available to them. Academics have studied intelligence techniques and have documented epic problems that have occurred when intelligence has gone wrong. For an enlightening white paper discussing intelligence challenges, I recommend "Assessing Uncertainty in Intelligence" by Jeffrey A. Friedman and Richard Zeckhauser.

When the Intel Is Wrong

Everyone knows intelligence can be wrong or unreliable. While I was stationed in Hawaii, we had tsunami warnings. An earthquake in Japan has the potential to cause a devastating tsunami all the way across the world.

Therefore, the local Hawaiian government uses Japanese earthquakes as a method for predicting tsunamis. The larger the earthquake, the more devastating the tsunami will likely be. However, several compounding variables can drastically change the impact of a tsunami. Sometimes the reports accurately predict devastating waves several feet tall; other times, when the tsunami waves hit, they are only inches tall.

Sirens built across the island are designed to warn residents when danger is coming; however, tsunamis are incredibly hard to predict. The responses of Hawaiian residents can vary considerably. Consistent false warnings of devastation can condition the residents to ignore the sirens. This can be dangerous, as a devastating tsunami can cause large amounts of damage and injure many residents. Therefore, the Hawaiian government takes great care to only provide a tsunami warning when they believe it is absolutely necessary, closely monitoring nearby islands to gather information to decide if they should sound the siren. If the siren is used too often, the residents won't respond, but missing just one warning may cost people their lives. With all the intelligence gathering, discussions, and apprehension about wave height, the best responses I have seen are locals using the siren to seek the high ground and hold a barbecue with friends.

The tsunami intelligence is parallel to threat intelligence because of all the compounding variables, which can lure people into a false sense of security. Similar to the "boy who cried wolf" scenario, security professionals will warn that the worst is coming and brace for impact, only to see an underwhelming threat or perhaps never see it at all.

Many of us know about the professional running around claiming that the whole data center will come crashing down and hackers are disassembling the Internet. During small outages, there are outrageous claims that being targets of APTs (advanced persistent threats) can explain power outages, erratic mouse movements, and unplugged Ethernet cables. Simple problems due to poor change management or user error can create large and expensive projects that do not make a safer network.

Companies selling software solutions help feed into this hype as well. Often vendors will claim they have a perfect threat-intelligence solution for all groups—the product that will solve all problems and ensure that the company is always one step ahead of the hackers. In reality, I have never seen this level of certainty in intelligence, except in manufactured scenarios and war games.

With all the good that threat intelligence can offer, and all the traps to make mistakes on, it is very likely the intelligence you receive will fall somewhere in the middle.

So make sure you verify all of your leads, remember when the information was wrong before, and do not go all in to one solution.

The Bias of Hindsight and the Risk of Overfitting

The often-cited and just as easily forgotten topic of hindsight demands constant refresher courses. Hindsight bias, or seeing an event as predictable despite little or no objective basis, can be devastating. Most notably it can blind you to objective consideration of security. If password misuse caused the last breach, woe to the executive who allows another password breach. Even more woe to their IT staff.

The danger with hindsight bias is it can lead an organization to protect against the last threat instead of the next one. The minor password infraction might have been embarrassing; however, it could be a large feint for a more vulnerable web server. Perhaps the denial of service could be a cover for an employee stealing large amounts of data. These examples demonstrate how limited resources could be diverted into protecting the wrong asset. Proper threat intelligence helps ensure that resources are going where they are needed.

Hindsight bias can also cause some emotional reactions. Technology is difficult to understand, but this can be forgotten during the heat of the moment when funding, clients, and jobs are being threatened. While a single incorrect prediction looks like a mistake, multiple recurrences of the same event look like failure and ineptitude. Inherently, managers know and understand this. Thus, organizations take action to ensure that, if another breach does occur, it at least does not occur the same way it did before. This can lead to some "security theater" in which individuals may show overly ambitious controls to mitigate low or even nonexistent risks.

An additional problem seen when setting up mitigations for past events is setting up controls to read signals that are not there. The term *oversetting* describes placing more reliance on a piece of information than should be placed. However, this doesn't mean lightning won't strike twice. If someone just stole money from your company, why wouldn't he or she try to do the exact same thing again? One of my favorite exercises to do as a pentester was to just start with the same exploits from the previous attempt.

Hindsight is a powerful tool to learn from past mistakes and prevent events from happening again. However, properly understanding a potential bias can help ensure that remediations are made relative to their risk, not their hype.

Threat Intelligence Understood

Understanding information about adversaries can create unique threat intelligence that can be used to protect an individual, company, or organization. The needs for intelligence are unique to every group, which determines the information that can be turned into intelligence and what can be discarded. As there are many methods to collect and distribute information, a threat-intelligence program needs to ensure that it is getting information to create intelligence that is actionable, consistent, and timely.

Summary

1. What is threat intelligence?
2. How is information different from intelligence?
3. What are some ways you can tell if you have good threat intelligence?
4. Why are models important for threat intelligence?
5. What are some ways in which threat intelligence can be collected?
6. How can threat intelligence be distributed?
7. What is the relationship between gathering threat intelligence and its usefulness?
8. What are three aspects of threat intelligence that make it useful?
9. What are some difficulties with threat intelligence? How can you mitigate these?

This section is designed to test understanding with a rather Socratic method.

Questions for Consideration

A friend at another company states he is seeing strange IP traffic in his network. The traffic comes from an area you do not do business in, and you do not see the traffic in your network.

1. What do you ask and tell your friend?
2. What do you do in your environment?
3. Who else do you share this information with?

The CIO has purchased a threat feed from a vendor. The feed sends all indicators in a weekly PDF. However, most of the indicators have already changed by publication.

1. Which of the three tenets for good threat intelligence does this violate?
2. What are some questions you can ask the vendor to make them better?

2

Implementing Threat Intelligence

Now that we have explored a definition of threat intelligence and how you can obtain it, let us explore how you can implement it to make your technology environment safer.

Understanding Your Environment

Understanding a technology environment can be one of the simplest and yet most overwhelming tasks you will ever be asked to accomplish. The edges showing where one technology ends and another begins continue to blur. Despite the difficulties, understanding the environment is the most important step to implement and utilize your threat-intelligence program. Without this step there is a real danger of miscategorizing threat and risk to your company.

If you have no idea what you are defending, how can you defend it? If you are watching all the exits but don't know about an equal number of hidden doors, are you really protecting your network? With firewalls, proxies, e-mails, mobile applications, wireless access points, and legacy systems, there are many, many ways for bad guys to misuse your network. On top of that, well-intentioned employees will plug in smartphones, load their favorite YouTube channels, click silly links on LinkedIn, and alter your network to unintentionally make defending the environment more difficult.

Knowing what the environment looks like now, what it will be designed to look like in the future, and how these transitions will occur is valuable. While your network might have a constantly shifting maze of opening and closing ports, it is possible to understand the major segments. Mapping the needs of these various segments and the users who depend on the technologies leads to a greater understanding.

Use-Case Models

The simplest method to understand your network will be to reverse your network into use-case models. Key considerations with these models should focus on the interactions between technologies and user groups.

The use-case models are an easy way to show responsibilities among different groups and people. They allow a quick assessment of what types of indicators are present. They also illustrate important threat-intelligence indicators that should be implemented.

When I build a diagram, I like to explore three things:

1. What does this system or technology do?
2. How does this system or technology interact with others?
3. Who is responsible for the system or technology?

It is important to note that I'm not really breaking the network down to the level of individual devices but rather into very large categories of function. This expands my understanding of the environment and identifies information needs. The high-level view keeps everything simple and easy to understand. For the purpose of understanding, more technical details would be distracting and add little value at this stage.

Knowing the larger overall structure allows an intelligence analyst to understand what kinds of information will be valuable to gather. Threat analysts can see where valuable assets may reside and the technologies supporting it. Patterns can emerge demonstrating which technology assets are essential to the operation of the business and which are less important. Additionally, this type of diagram can quickly be shown to the correct stakeholders to help drive a decision.

There is often resistance to completing this task; however, the ability of an analyst to communicate properly is the catalyst for transforming information into intelligence. For example, if a threat actor is targeting cloud services, and you have identified a distinct group that deals with cloud services, you can send information directly to the responsible party. Keeping communication at the logical level allows for the major interactions to take place on rapid timelines.

When developing your use-case models, try to identify information that would be valuable for the people in those sectors. But most importantly, ask them what information they want and will use in a crisis. Updating your diagram can help resolve this issue. By creating a succinct diagram, discovering connection mechanisms, and determining responsibility for components, you can get a good idea of how to better build threat intelligence and provide actionable intelligence to the right people. Nobody has the time to sift through information they do not need, so don't waste anyone's time by collecting information nobody reads.

Technical Network Maps

Tailored intelligence is exactly what many people are interested in when they are building a threat-intelligence program. Once you have drilled down some strategic high-level objectives identified by the use-cases, you may determine that a more detailed technical network map is needed. This more detailed map would include individual machines, addresses, ports, and protocols across the environment. More succinct information allows an analyst to pay close attention to the details in the network.

After building a realistic model, I like to compare it with the findings from vulnerability scans and penetration tests. This is my preferred method because there are often ports, protocols, services, and IPs that have been supposedly discontinued or disabled, only to sit dormant for years. These omissions can be juicy targets for threat actors. Pentesting allows you to "trust but verify" that the network appears as you thought it would. Discovering unexpected results can alter how you weigh threat intelligence, and findings will likely force you to recheck your model to better meet the needs of your new environment.

Realistically, intelligence defined down to such a technical level is rare. Also, there are diminishing returns as you try to find that last 10 percent of services, hosts, and networks. The additional details take time, and some details can change rapidly. Hence, I find 60 to 90 percent coverage is a good range to make threat-intelligence decisions. You know enough about the network to invest time and effort on products without wasting time on isolated, esoteric processes.

Overall, I have not found this level of specific detail to be particularly helpful to me. The details I can provide do not match the granularity that feeds provide. If you are getting intelligence drilled down to the exact targets, personas, and IPs targeting your company, please reach out to me. I need to learn your ways.

Priority Categorization

What are your most important applications for the business? If you just ask someone, he or she will likely simply state, "All of these applications are essential to generating a product." However, as we all know, this is rarely the case. Some applications are essential to continuing the operation of the business, and some can go offline for weeks before being noticed.

I like to reframe the question for the business user and ask, "If today you could only use one program, what would it be?" Then find the next one and then the next one until you have a list of applications in order of importance. This helps you set a priority on what is important and what you should spend time gathering threat information on.

During a war game, or even at the beginning of an incident, you can use this list to make sure the company's priorities haven't changed. You will be surprised how a month later priorities may have become completely different.

I prefer to group them together in similar categories and similar priorities. My high-priority web applications will require different actions than lower-priority network problems. The threats to my web applications will be approximately the same level but are likely distinctly different from the threats to networks.

Understanding Control Implementation

How do we implement such a thing? There seems to be a correlation between how easy it is to spot something and how easy it is to change it.

Precise intelligence would know that a man wearing a blue shirt would be stealing your wallet at 2:00 p.m. from your desk. This blue-shirt intelligence meets our requirements of timeliness, certainty, and actionability. A defender knows exactly what to look for, when to look for it, and where to look. After you've received this intelligence, if your wallet was still stolen from your desk at 2:00 p.m., I would be disappointed in you. However, it is rarely that easy. Most threat intelligence is rather vague and general. Knowing that someone with a shirt will steal something from your town on Sunday is not as good threat intelligence. Let's break down why.

- The time frame is larger and less succinct. Instead of being prepared at a specific time, you would have to be vigilant over a longer period.
- The target is also nebulous. With the wallet, we knew exactly what they were going for, and we could move it or secure it accordingly.
- The area is large. Your desk can be monitored more easily than the entire town.

Every defensive function requires a certain amount of resources to accomplish. These defensive actions are often referred to as controls, or items that make the environment safer. As the level of ambiguity rises, the commitment of time, money, and resources for these controls also increases. In the vague example just described, you would need to hire guards for longer hours, hire more guards to look after more items, and cover a bigger area. There is always a price for defense. Sometimes it is manpower, electricity, or processing speed of functions, but there is always a price to pay for control.

The single greatest reason to cultivate good intelligence is the ability to implement controls and therefore use fewer resources. By being specific, threat intelligence can be implemented easily and effectively.

How to Put It in Place

So you have built out all kinds of sources, indicators, and this great information repository. What are some examples in which controls are used to protect an environment?

I have created a short list of the most common ideas that are used across all environments.

Whitelisting and Blacklisting

Whitelisting and blacklisting are certainly the most common methods for adding threat intelligence into your environment. Blocking IPs and URLs is easy to implement and has been done for quite some time. It is a great way to reduce the attack surface of the network.

There are multiple ways to do this.

1. Blacklisting: Blocking IPs and URLs by address block or domain. This can be done for a variety of reasons. Perhaps you don't have any legitimate business in country X. Blocking traffic to that destination reduces an unnecessary attack surface.

2. Whitelisting: Allowing access to only specific addresses. This method is time-consuming because it requires stakeholders to let the environment know about the services they are using. If new services are needed, they will need to be unblocked.

3. Just-in-time whitelisting: As malicious indicators are received, the indicators are compared against a business need. If no business need is identified, the indicator is blocked. At first glance this seems like an appropriate method. The problem becomes similar to whitelisting. You don't know there is a business impact until the indicator is investigated.
4. Block and hope: Feeding entire lists into devices in an automated fashion to block IPs and *hope* it doesn't impact the business. My old skipper told me, "Hope is never a course of action," but many people try it anyway.

Blocking is best seen in a tactical sense. It can be done quickly, which might be extremely important to stop an ongoing attack.

Generating Alerts

Many devices can set up alerts that are sent to incident responders if certain actions are seen in the network. Using threat indicators to trigger alerts in your environment is similar to blocking but will not disrupt business functions or ongoing attacks. While alerts do not stop an attack in progress, alerts let a responder know if something interesting is happening. Many security devices set up alerts automatically using indicators drawn from proprietary information.

You could generate alerts for

- Going to an IP
- Visiting a URL
- Uncharacteristic behavior
- Known malicious indicators

If an analyst has the ability to create custom signatures based off specific threat information, we have a mechanism to serve the unique needs of the business.

One of the difficulties with this method is being able to properly tune alerts. Too many alerts and an analyst will be overworked and unsure of what to do. Too few and you are letting the bad guys through.

Monitoring and Incident Response

My favorite use of threat information is to enable better threat monitoring and incident response. Almost all security analysts use threat intelligence in some form; they just might be using it informally. Providing analysts with access to new, relevant information can help save them time researching and can help expedite recovery. More importantly, providing analysts intelligence allows them to better understand what they are seeing in the environment. They can understand relationships to past incidents and what information they *need* in order to make better decisions in their investigation.

Determining which groups of information are useful to security analysts will be unique to each company. The important part is the communication aspect. Understanding what is useful to the responder and sharing the information allows insight into the threat landscape, and seeing how threats operate allows you to get ahead of them.

Hunting and a Hunt Program

Building a hunt team is becoming popular in the threat-intelligence world. Proactively searching for interesting threat information can help a SOC (security operations center) detect new threats and problems. Sometimes information from hunting can detect something that has been in the environment for years. A successful hunt is lots of fun, and executives love it. Analysts enjoy bringing back a trophy of something they found.

Hunt programs can also be designed to look for threat intelligence. When discussing a hunt program, I like considering where my hunting grounds are. I like to separate hunting into two factions:

- External to the company environment
- Internal to the company environment

Hunting for information external to the environment can be a popular tactic. Bad guys are everywhere and doing interesting things all the time. Researching them for indicators can lead in many interesting directions, including underground and clandestine organizations. However, with all this exploring, you do run into questions of authority. Should you attempt to connect to a malicious website with a sandbox? Should you be purchasing stolen documents to look for company credentials? Overall I tend to feel that research companies and government/law enforcement best do this type of activity, because it quickly gets into areas of vague legality and violating personal privacy.

Internal hunting is similar in that you are moving around the environment looking for things that are suspicious. However, it is different because you own the infrastructure. Internal hunting is usually going to net a higher benefit for your organization. If you see something in your environment, you know it will be attacking your environment or has already attacked it. Conversely, external threats may never intend to attack you. Therefore, it makes sense to concentrate on strange behavior in your environment and match it up with what is happening outside, rather than solving external problems to prevent them internally.

A great hunt team will be able to notice anomalies and inefficiencies in the network. This indication that something is amiss can be numerous things. Although it could be the next APT breaking down your door, it can also be a misconfigured server. That's not to say that aspect should be ignored; instead, if you can document it and show it to the process owners, you can help make the whole system better.

Devices

More specifically, where can we implement fixes in the network? Various devices each have unique uses that can be enhanced by threat-intel indicators.

Firewalls!

We love firewalls, right? And now they can do more and more. Initially firewalls just provided some access-control lists and blocking. Now we see them implementing additional protection measures. More and more features keep getting added into firewalls, and threat intelligence is no exception. While some allow simple text files to be added, a few more on the horizon are working on ingesting automated threat feeds using STIX and TAXII.

Network Intrusion-Detection Systems (NIDS)

Network intrusion-detection systems provide a review of traffic on the network to properly protect it. NIDS sensors are typically placed in the network observing traffic either in-line or parallel. Certain traffic patterns are identified as malicious and will alert responders on discovery. Threat intelligence can be used to help build unique patterns to put in place with a NIDS system.

Host-Based Intrusion-Detection System (HIDS)/Endpoint Solutions

Most host-based detection systems are thought of as simple antivirus solutions. They have been around for quite some time where known bad files will be blocked, alerted, and quarantined if they are detected. However, endpoint solutions have been very simplistic for the most part, often using proprietary updates and feeds to prevent something from running in the environment.

New versions of endpoint solutions include detection devices and agents that are constantly running to detect hashes, behaviors, changes in registry keys, and references to known hooking/injecting spots, which denote they are being malicious. Similar to NIDS systems, several are trying to include methods to add in threat intelligence manually or through automated fields.

Web Proxies and Web-Application Firewalls

Several interesting systems are used to protect applications. Proxies can help protect the environment by obscuring the systems connecting out to the Internet.

A proxy also allows for a chokepoint so you can put in threat intelligence to stop malicious traffic. If you know a certain domain is hosting malicious sites and has no business need, you can ensure that traffic reaching out through the proxy is blocked.

Web-application firewalls (WAF) can offer something similar. They provide sound defense from web-based attack, from users browsing to malicious sites, and even from pieces of code communicating with each other.

Mobile

Mobile security is something new that is popping up over and over again. The dependence of employees on phones has helped drive this. Several types of clever malware have been used with the Android and OS X operating systems.

Most protection relies on the installation of special software to isolate private and company information from other system processes. Additionally, some of these solutions can route traffic back through the company's network to help restrict malicious or dangerous sites.

Therefore, threat intel tends to be added to network devices over individual platforms.

Tactics Versus Strategy

The security world's use of the terms *tactics* and *strategy* can vary greatly from one group to the next. The terms *tactical* and *strategic* are poorly defined in most IT literature. In fact, the best definitions I have found describing these terms are in the military Joint Planning Publication JP 3-13. However, since vendors continue to use these words interchangeably, we will quickly cover the differences a threat analyst should remember.

Tactical actions are, in short, quick actions that are often temporary or a Band-Aid fix. Strategic actions are long, extended actions that create lasting changes. However, they take time and money to complete correctly. Typically, a strategic goal is composed of several smaller tactical goals.

While there is also an operational level, it acts as an intermediary between strategic and tactical.

Tactical Intelligence

Tactics are very low-level operations that quickly change and are often temporal. If you are dealing with individuals or small organizations, you are dealing with tactical decisions. Some networking actions I consider tactical include blocking IPs, searching a small subset of logs, and doing any activity that can be conceived and executed within one day. Normally, tactical actions are conducted below the management level.

Since many intelligence concepts come from military or law enforcement, the term *tactical* comes with exciting imagery. It invokes comparison with SWAT teams and special-operations teams responding quickly to a bank robbery or combat raid. This imagery is why many groups try to label more intelligence as tactical. It just feels cool.

One problem with tactical operations is that quick reactions can result in things going very wrong. Imagine blocking the company's payroll service, Google, or regulatory reporting feeds. All of these tactical-level mistakes can be costly. Therefore, if your organization is using intelligence to quickly make changes in the environment, it should be practiced beforehand and be well documented. After all, if you want that "cool tactical SWAT team" vibe, you need to practice, practice, and practice so mistakes aren't made.

Strategic Intelligence

Strategic intelligence deals with much larger operations and movements. Typically, strategic thinking guides an entire company policy for months or years. Some examples of strategy are business plans, implementing new hardware changes, massive network rearchitectures, and building out a security team. All these actions take time, most take money, and many evolve from their initial plans.

While not as shiny and cool as tactical operations, strategic IT changes offer some of the best defenses and improvements for a network. Building a multitiered network takes time, money, and resources. However, once it is complete, the strategic project can free up system resources and essential personnel to work on other problems found throughout a network. Finding the right people to build out a defense team also takes time and resources. Training new people can be a huge time sink, pulling away some of your best people from the important bits of technology. However, once completed, it can free up those same people to do amazing things.

Trying to make a change while continuing operations makes strategic thought even more difficult. People change out roles, and new technologies come online, while old ones become laden with more vulnerabilities and incompatibility issues. Last-minute emergencies steal time away from individuals and their strategic objectives on an almost daily basis. Realizing that strategic goals often are neglected for the present day, it is important to ensure that strategic goals remain aligned with company objectives and continue to progress.

Despite all these difficulties, a well-thought-out strategic plan can pay huge dividends when your responders need to react to a crisis in the early morning or track down a breach.

Types of Threat Actors

As the use of technology increases, the number of threat actors misusing the technology follows suit. Criminal gangs, hacktivists, nation-states, and others have all shown intent and ability to exploit new technologies to further their own agendas. Understanding the motives, composition, and goals of threat actors is a cornerstone in having a successful threat-intelligence program.

Hacktivists

Hacktivists are driven by ideals and fame more than money. Typically, hacktivists have been known to target just one company or person to prove their point or promote a belief.

The group "Lizard Squad" is an interesting example of hacktivists. Not only has Lizard Squad taken down the Sony PlayStation network several times, they have also caused havoc in other interesting ways. In 2014, the group executed a DDoS, which took down the Sony network for several hours and called in a bomb threat, which diverted a Sony executive's plane.

How to gather intel on hacktivists: Hacktivists typically try to recruit members through the use of social media and need to coordinate on public channels. There are many ways to monitor these types of public feeds to see the precursors to hacktivist attacks and recruiting efforts and influence what they are targeting. While each group is unique, public Twitter accounts, IRC channels, and chat programs are common tools activists use to coordinate.

Due to their open nature, hacktivists are rather easy to infiltrate. Many security companies exploit this weakness and try to embed people in private chat rooms in order to monitor their activities. Being part of these channels can lead to useful information when dealing with a public hacktivist group.

Additionally, hacktivists are looking for recognition and will publicly advertise the attacks they will be attempting and signal when they will occur. If hacktivists attempt to deface a website, they let everyone know their intentions before they launch their attacks. Being able to see this information ahead of time gives the analyst an opportunity to fight back against the attack before it even starts.

Due to the decentralized nature of the threat, many people will claim responsibility for hacks or claim to represent bigger groups than they do. For example, there is no "Anonymous" but rather groups of people who claim to speak on its behalf. Therefore, indicators from one "Anonymous" operation might or might not be the same across groups.

The Criminal Element

Criminals have gotten extremely complex in recent years. Until recently, crimes relied on computer fraud on a small scale. A few small attackers enjoyed a niche market in which they could steal personnel information and funds. However, today entire infrastructures are based off criminal businesses that steal company data for profit. These professional criminals have exploit-development teams, money-laundering teams, malware-delivery teams, spam teams, and so on. This increasingly specialized business model creates an interesting problem. How often are you up against a business actively trying to break in and steal money from you?

For example, the Carbanak group is currently stealing millions of dollars from banks by breaking into their systems. Members of Carbanak have multiple objectives to accomplish on their targets. They are infiltrating security cameras to observe how the bank tellers act and are conducting transfers of company assets at odd intervals. They have people learn and understand every aspect of the victim bank's operation. These are several steps past the typical actions seen from common criminals.

How to gather intel on computer criminals: This new breed of criminals is harder to gather intel on because they tend not to communicate through open channels. Usually communication is through carefully vetted web services and forums. This has become more interesting in recent years. Like an underground Etsy, there are freelance malware writers, credit-card resellers, and botnet owners who sell and rent their stolen wares on underground markets.

Several intelligence groups try to embed themselves in these underground communities in order to gather information and make threat intelligence useful for organizations. This has mixed success among the different vendors, and I would urge you to consider the feeds they provide. Data widely vary from the vendors as well. Therefore, it is important to look at how the threat information would benefit your company.

Another method to gain insight on criminal procedures is to observe what is happening at peer organizations. The tactics of criminals can be similar, and knowing how they are impacting peers can help provide information about what you can do at your company.

Insider Threats

Insider threats are a fun topic. Everyone wants to think about how "their manager doesn't respect them" or how undervalued they are. Many more employees are stealing data as they move to another company and want to take their data with them. The problem is some people carry out these daydreams to make an extra buck or exact revenge on their companies. Since employees have unique accesses, insiders have already bypassed several protective layers defending the company from other threats.

Part of the difficulty in trying to research and mitigate insider threats is not wishing to offend employees or to overstep the fine line between diligent security professional and stalker. However, some sources claim that employee theft can account for as much as 5 percent of a company's revenue a year. With such a large percentage of revenue being stolen by insiders, to ignore this potential threat seems careless.

It will be difficult to determine where exactly information should be gathered to make good insider-threat intel. Investigations can quickly start if stolen documents are being released publicly or on social media. Some other classic examples of insider threats involve looking for strange behavior in the environment. Is one employee coming and going at strange hours? Are one employee's accounts being used in the middle of the night? Is a particular account using more bandwidth than the other users? Looking at the behavior associated with the employee in the workforce is probably the most accurate and well-tested avenue for investigating insider threat.

While company policies for investigating individuals vary greatly, if you are concentrating on a specific employee, the human-resources department should be contacted. It is important to involve them earlier in the process so policies are not violated while searching for a threat insider.

Insider threats are a difficult item to detect in a company because gathering information can be sensitive. Sharing information on how thefts might occur and knowing what new technology is available can help put procedures in place to detect and prevent these threats.

How to gather intel on insider threats: The best prevention for insider threats is to ensure that employees have some checks and balances to their job responsibilities. Alternatively, if they are in charge of a database, make sure other employees can also get to that database and alternative backups. Strange hours, a sudden influx of money, or bragging might signal that an insider is in the process of stealing or causing damage. Other abnormal behaviors like sudden weird hours or logging in at strange times can suggest a threat. Movement of large amounts of data or requesting access to information outside of the scope of their work are good indicators that people are looking to get information and access they do not need.

Accusing employees of stealing confidential information is difficult because it can create a sense of mistrust between the managers and employees. However, many of the mitigations for insider threat, such as segmentation and least privilege, are also good defensive postures for security breaches. Using this angle can help soften the accusatory nature of mitigations.

Competitors

Industrial espionage is rapidly becoming more common. The United States does enjoy some unique privileges in preventing competitors from stealing proprietary data; however, other countries do not abide by the same rules and laws. Global competitors may try to steal information, and some view it as another aspect of doing business.

There are many avenues through which information can be stolen. Insiders can simply sell information to competitors. Longer espionage activities can involve groups working in an organization for years and slowly siphoning data to competitors. Perhaps one of the most surprising trends in the last three years is the amount of research-development data being stolen from colleges, overseas manufacturing plants, and even government groups.

How to gather intel on company espionage: Much like insider threats, company espionage is difficult to detect and attribute. It takes a lot of skill to determine where the stolen information is sent, and information is often impossible to recover when an attack is successful. While similar designs and watermarking important properties can hint toward overseas competitors stealing information, it is difficult to prevent. The best solutions are similar to those of the insider threat. Monitoring employees and conducting background checks can be valuable in causing them to resort to different tactics.

Advanced Persistent Threats (APTs)

An advanced persistent threat (APT) is a term thrown around frequently. Highlighted as some of the most fearsome hacking groups, APTs are simply threat actors discovered by security companies while investigating incidents. While APTs may seem fearsome due to their association with very public incidents, many APTs are simply extremely persistent but not very advanced.

The important distinction I make is that an APT will keep going after a determined target to meet its goals and has the resources to do so for a very long time.

APTs are often more organized then many other threat actors and in some instances connected with nation-states. This sponsorship gives APTs a far greater pool of resources to wage an attack over a much longer campaign. More personnel, more funding, more training, more equipment, and possibly even leverage into telecommunications companies can make APTs very difficult to protect against. This massive amount of resources and influence is daunting to any type of defender.

Another difficulty with APTs is their larger array of potential attacks and attack vectors. Hacktivists can become bored, insider threats can be fired, and criminals will search for different suckers, but an APT can wait it out. They can change their tactics, probe, and plot, and it is unlikely they will stop if you have the information they want. For you as a defender, APTs are scary because they can keep coming for years, and you can't fail once.

How to gather intel on APTs: Gathering information on APTs can be very difficult because they are not sharing their stolen information or the tools they have developed. Internal communication isn't conducted on public channels, and it's hard for a security company to embed into their organization. APTs may have the resources to develop or purchase unique exploits that they keep among their teams. Therefore, any APT information will likely only be discovered during an investigation of a breach. Security-research companies tend to be the best providers of this information, since they are in the unique position of seeing APT indicators while responding to a client's incident.

Luckily, APT information is often disclosed by a government organization wishing to limit the APTs' impact on local companies. Information feeds from InfraGard, Department of Homeland Security, and US-Cert are great resources that gather information from APT breaches against US companies. Reaching out to industry peer groups is also a common practice allowing researchers to compare the notes or tactics of threats they see every day.

New Threat Actors

Although this is a good list of threat actors, it is far from complete. Every industry has unique and specific actors requiring more defined roles and investigations to prevent threats. Therefore, when looking at new threat actors and their abilities, try to remember three questions:

1. What is their mission?
2. What do they look like on the network?
3. Why would they target you and how?

If you can answer these three questions, you are well on your way to effectively mitigating them as a threat.

A large problem often discussed is how motivations of individuals change based on culture. My resources, background, lifestyle, and family values are much different from those of a scam artist in Africa. To apply the same techniques and draw similar conclusions without understanding their culture can invite incorrect bias to your threat-intelligence data.

Threat-Actor Conclusion

Dealing with hacktivists, criminals, APTs, and others while keeping up with the latest technologies is tough. However, by understanding the motives, composition, and goals of threat actors, a good threat-intelligence program will be able to slow them down.

Pyramid of Pain

I first saw this concept explained by David Bianco with a post dating back to 2013. The Pyramid of Pain is possibly the simplest way to show that all indicators are not created equal. Starting from the bottom and going to the top, you have:

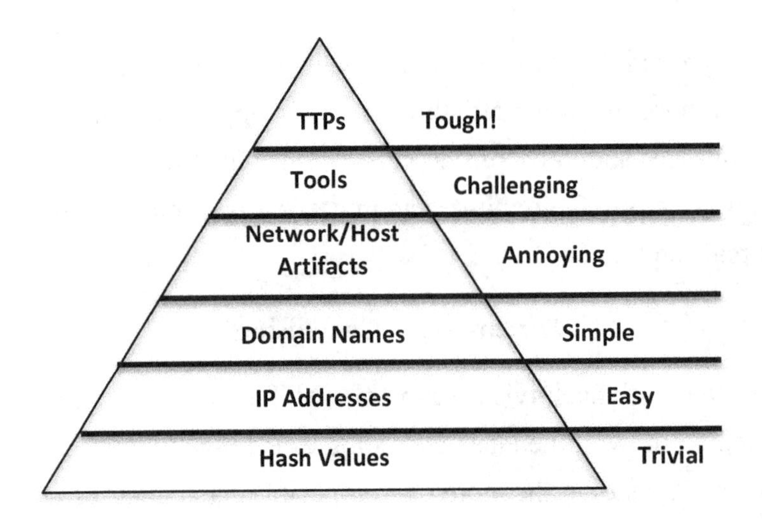

- Hash values: the fingerprint of a program (MD5s, SHA1s)
- IP addresses: the address for C2 communication
- Domain names: used for delivery or C2 communication (URIs and URLs)
- Network/host artifacts: things are left behind in the registry (registry keys, files)
- Tools: software used to conduct attacks (NMAP, scripts, specific malware)
- TTPs: types of delivery (spearphishing, whaling, web attacks, SQL injections)

As you read through this list, you will notice that the identifiers become more difficult as you go down the list. However, the easy-to-use identifiers are also easy for an attacker to change. This creates an interesting dynamic for threat analysts when determining the value of using different indicators.

Hash Values

Hash values provide a fingerprint for files, allowing rapid comparison. In my experience, the most prevalent threat data with hashes are MD5s, and these are a great example of indicators because they are extremely easy to use. Certain software can fingerprint every file on a computer, so it can determine if one malicious file is also being used in other locations.

If anything alters the file, the hash value also changes. This can be problematic, since an attacker is likely using many files. The list of MD5 files associated with an attacker is often immense. Sometimes the lists of associated hash values can be pages upon pages long. These large amounts of indicators can be prohibitively difficult to manage.

Additionally, attackers concerned about attribution through MD5s could simply alter their files to generate a unique MD5 for each stage and method of their attack. Furthermore, the research paper "How to Break MD5 and Other Hash Functions" by Xiaoyun Wang and Hongbo Yu outlines a specific method demonstrating how malicious users can change MD5s to impersonate other files on the same system. Therefore, the relative ease with which MD5s could be gathered as threat indicators is tempered by their relative ease of being changed.

IP Addresses/Domain Names

IP addresses and domain names are often the favorite threat indicators. Network administrators understand how to use a firewall and can block the IP traffic easily, and analysts can use an IP address to prevent traffic from one particular source. Domain names can also be blocked in a similar fashion. Using either indicator can be executed quickly as well, which is perfect in the middle of an attack.

IPs and domains can still be easily used and discarded by both malware and criminals. If an indicator is blocked, they can shift to a new one. Shifting between addresses is also seen in malware to increase resilience and ensure that if one pathway is blocked, another is available. Attribution can also be complicated because at the source of the traffic could be other compromised computers, free Internet hotspots, or anonymization by some other means.

Network/Host Artifacts

Tools are extremely interesting to play with. Many hacktivists have fired up the Low Orbit Ion Cannon (LOIC) to run denial-of-service attacks, and almost every security person has experience with Kali Linux (formerly

Backtrack). However, APTs and malware authors also use specially built tools to help them complete their objectives more quickly. Many APTs have their own personal subsets that they prefer.

Finding specific tools like this can be a great indicator of which threat actors you are dealing with. If a threat actor uses a certain tool, you can place additional constraints on using it or perhaps investigate if you can remove it from the environment. You would be surprised what you can get rid of. Of course, a dedicated threat will simply shift their toolset, but some groups, like hacktivists, might not be able to recreate a tool.

Tactics, Techniques, and Procedures

Tactics, techniques, and procedures involve noticing how the threat behaves. There are examples showing that criminal groups from certain areas will only be working during a certain time frame. If traffic is seen in eight-hour shifts, for six days in a row, it might suggest the criminals are an organized group. Attacks occurring during the weekends or holidays suggest attackers are using their free time. This is important for a few reasons. If you can notice when a group operates, you might be able to place additional restrictions and mitigations during those times. Perhaps have shorter logout times or block certain domains during their heightened hours.

A fantastic example of a TTP was with the Anthem and Premera breaches. These large health-care organizations both saw similar TTP indicators using similar domain names going outside of their organization. The intelligence indicators from Anthem were used by Premera to find this malicious domain and start responding to the incident.

Not all indicators are created equal. By looking up and down the "Pyramid of Pain," threat analysts can use the ones most appropriate to their investigation and intelligence gathering.

Using Metrics to Measure What You Value

There is little value in what you cannot measure. The value of metrics and gathering data is often discussed in-depth in the literature. Entire businesses revolve around finding, parsing, and spewing information. Luckily for the threat analyst, spigots of information are plentiful. Unfortunately, most people are drowning in the overabundance of information. Two types of measurement—qualitative and quantitative—are the first strokes in learning to swim in this information tide.

Qualitative information demonstrates the quality of the measure. Stating how green the sea is, how soft a bed is, or how safe a network is are all very qualitative. It provides an example of how things are on a spectrum.

There might be many different interpretations of the qualitative terms, and this ambiguity can harm the threat intelligence process. Imagine an intel analyst discovering information that suggests a threat actor is talented, well resourced, or dangerous. Would a different analyst measure the threat actor the same way? What exactly does the analyst mean by "well resourced," and can you compare how "well resourced" one threat is to another? A threat program needs to have answers for these questions if analysts are to standardize the qualitative aspect of their intelligence.

Qualitative terms are acceptable for broad statements and are easily gathered. But there are often instances in which you need to decide between defending against two or more "major threats," and you will need additional information in order to choose which one is worse.

Quantitative information determines the numbers associated with a measurement. Stating that there are thirty-plus people, incidents have increased 34 percent, or the boat is on forty feet of water are all quantitative measures.

Quantitative metrics are convenient because everything is countable and demonstrable. It is much easier for several analysts to provide the same information about the number of breaches and to show their work if they disagree.

Qualitative measurements often seem to carry less weight, because they can be subjective among the different people in the room. Therefore, getting quantitative numbers to help support qualitative statements is helpful when communicating that threat intelligence is properly scoped and received.

Gathering Useful Metrics for a Safer Environment

One way many people can relate to threat intelligence is to compare how similar it is to gathering metrics in other aspects of business. From sales to employee evaluations, everything seeks to gather information regarding a subject. If sales numbers are below average, the company response might be to start an investigation. If a company notices that a customer's satisfaction rating is significantly lower than normal, the customer might be contacted to remediate the problem. These methods of finding a problem and then responding should be emulated in threat intelligence.

People can also use metrics to further their own goals. Gathering metrics to justify your job, program, or new projects is a tempting and quite common practice. It is easy to demonstrate that projects are being completed, money is being spent, and warm bodies are in seats. It is much harder to gather metrics demonstrating that the environment is getting safer. Despite the difficulty, it is important to concentrate on what you are trying to measure instead of what is easy to measure.

When developing quantitative metrics for a threat-intelligence program, ensure that the information gathered has established thresholds for action. If incidents increase by 50 percent, perhaps you hire additional employees to help handle incidents. If the number of unique threat actors from a region triples, you can reevaluate the security posture of that area. Without establishing thresholds, it is less likely that a decision will ever be made, and all your efforts will just be extra work.

Is This Worth It?

Despite the difficulties, metrics can be a great way to show higher management what your team has accomplished and what you are going to accomplish. With threat intel, I would look at some easy wins:

- Number of attacks stopped
- Number of criminals detected
- Number of indicators seen in the networks
- Number of incidents prevented

By chaining gathered information together, you can come up with compelling narratives, for example, like this one: *This year our intelligence program prevented X files from being exfiltrated. Losing these files would have cost the* *company $Y. Our budget used to gain this information was $Z. Therefore, our return on investment was $Y/Z.*

Giving simple, transparent numbers can help push the narrative forward. Just about any businessperson can see if there is value added if the information is communicated in a style they are accustomed to.

Unfortunately, the numbers will not always be in your favor. In these circumstances, it might be tempting to concentrate on other numbers that look better. Sometimes the actions taken from threat intelligence did not make the environment safer, but slowed work and presented new vulnerabilities. These scenarios aren't the end of the world. It's okay to fail and catch it early. Most people don't even consider not meeting metrics failing; rather, they consider it constructive learning of what works in the current environment.

Accurate metrics will help detect what you need to reinforce and what you need to cut back. Without having anything to measure about your program successes, your threat-intelligence program is similar to blind guesses.

Borrowing the Tools of Epidemiology

In 1854 John Snow was investigating why cholera outbreaks were occurring in the streets of London. By applying some broad metrics to track the location of the diseased population, he was able to determine the source of the infection: a small, local water pump. Soon after the discovery, the handle for the pump was removed, and the cholera outbreak quickly subsided. John Snow is considered one of the founding fathers of epidemiology due to his study of disease and because many of his techniques are still used today.

Modern malware may be viewed as similar to the 1854 London cholera outbreak in many ways. Finding the exact sources of infections is difficult, but through study and plotting of metrics, Snow was able to find the source. To draw a comparison, John Snow was studying the enemy, and that allowed him to stop the spread of it.

Part of the toolset Snow built required gathering enough data and then determining how good the data were. Testing data for epidemiologists is difficult on a large population, and the problem is only worse for threat analysts. Each employee is a massive communication highway of different bits and pieces of information. To help hunt down sources, consider attack rate, specificity, and sensitivity. These three tools can help measure whether your indicators are leading to the right track.

Attack rate: The number of people exposed to a source who develop symptoms. The number of people exposed divides this number.

For example, a phishing campaign sent one hundred e-mails to a company. The company had five users click the link (5/100 = 5% attack rate). We should suspect that if one e-mail campaign had a higher attack rate, the company had a worse exposure to the phishing e-mails.

Sensitivity: The number of positives that are correctly measured by the test.

For example, let us suppose one hundred machines are infected and a test is created to determine whether these computers are infected. If the sensitivity of the test were 70 percent, then around seventy machines would be identified as having an infection. The other thirty machines would still be infected and have a false negative result.

Specificity: The number of negatives that are correctly measured by the test.

For example, let's pretend twenty computers in a lab are suspected to have had malware removed from them. However, only nineteen have actually had the malware removed. The specificity rate would be 95 percent.

How to Use Sensitivity and Specificity

If your company is using a system to detect malware, it is important to track its sensitivity and specificity. By comparing these simple ratios, a valuable determination can be made of the effectiveness of the service. Try comparing them with other services to see which services work best for the environment.

Can Epidemiology Really Be Useful for Malware?

Unfortunately, some unique characteristics of malware make it different from the study of disease. Malware can reach much greater distances than diseases. Cholera is limited geographically, but the Internet reaches across the world. By these terms, the attack rate is very high for malware. The large numbers and rapid speed force us to compile information quickly, as the attack vector changes rapidly as well.

While this may seem daunting, tools already exist to rapidly pull and change data at massive scales. Therefore, it seems the biggest problem is being able to draw corollaries among these terms and seeing if they provide some relevance if they are applied to your business needs. We know epidemiology works. Some doctors dedicate their entire professional careers in this field to help save people's lives. Since they have about a 150-year head start on threat intelligence, I suggest stealing some of their terms, like sensitivity and specificity.

Metrics and the Value of Measuring Success

None of this information matters if you are not able to measure how successful you are at achieving your goals. Metrics are tough in any discipline but especially in threat intelligence. While you might borrow some tools and thoughts from epidemiology, the important part is communicating the information successfully to the other party.

How Threat Intelligence Changes over Time

Threat intelligence is not a static product. Like a twisted garden, it grows, changes, and needs constant review over time. When considering different time frames, an analyst can create completely different uses that are all worth exploring. For ease of use, I will discuss how MD5s and IPs may change over time for a hacktivist threat actor in three ways, using the indicators in the past, present, and future.

Looking into the Past (after an Incident)

Searching through logs for indicators of attacks and threat vectors is the absolute and most common use of threat intelligence. The logic of looking through past incidents is highly apparent to most people in the IT world.

When searching through incidents in the past, we know the attack has already happened. As long as there is good logging, there is nothing a threat actor can do to change their past indicators. There is no taking back tactics, tool usage, or IPs used to communicate home. Those bits and pieces of information will always be there. When an IP address is hardcoded into malware, even if the IP address is changed in the future, there is the information that the IP was used in the past. However, it is an entirely different matter if those indicators were properly logged and stored by recording tools.

Since indicators cannot be retroactively changed, threat actors confuse researchers by attacking recording tools. Avoiding detection and disrupting logging tools are taught in fundamental penetration-testing courses. Threat actors can disable, obfuscate, corrupt, or alter logs to hinder the use of past indicators. Because of this, defenders are challenged with maintaining a set of logs detailed enough to allow attribution to malicious actions.

While researching indicators in the past allows the best understanding of what has happened, it does not protect from the damage that has already occurred. The damage is done. Wanting to prevent damage, the community has shifted to a more proactive stance. We look toward using indicators in the present or perhaps in the future to prevent damage to the IT infrastructure.

Looking at the Present (at the Time of Incident)

Knowing an IP or MD5 is currently in the environment demonstrates that something needs to be dealt with immediately. There is even a sense of emergency, since at this stage defenders will be able to help stop or mitigate the damage from attackers. Actions taken during this stage can directly stop something bad from happening or minimize the damage that is occurring.

If you discover suspicious IPs on an infected host, most likely other groups (internal or external to the company) are seeing similarly suspicious behavior. This fresh information linking strange new behaviors prompts responders to gather additional information. Behavior seen in one area should be quickly investigated in another. Present intel is best used in an incident response where some information was brought to the attention of the responders and can be used for quicker remediations elsewhere.

Intelligence at this stage brings about a spy versus spy. The threat actor can change indicators if responders spook them. If attackers feel as if their current activities are drawing attention, they can drop out of their operations, close things down, and prevent further discovery of their tactics and techniques. Attackers would only suspect this if the environment changes, an IP address or process keeps being killed immediately, a custom signature appears on the virus total, or other offensive intelligence gathering is done.

An additional determination could be made for weighing the impact of the attacker's continued operations against the intelligence benefit to responders for studying the attacker's behavior. Hence, as a team enacts real-time threat intelligence, it is important to follow best practices for incident remediation and have a plan in place for these scenarios.

Predicting the Future (Getting Ahead of the Incident)

The future is a much more problematic time frame to work in because every indicator can change without provocation. Threat actors don't have to be spooked to change indicators. Threats can decide to periodically switch IPs or improve their malware (which will change the associated MD5). Especially as the intelligence becomes dated, it becomes more difficult to predict what a threat actor will do in the future.

Therefore, I feel IPs and MD5s would be a bad fit for attempting to detect and block the same threat actor moving forward. They are inadvertently or purposely changed too often to get usable feedback. However, as threat analysts, we can solve this by moving up the Pyramid of Pain. MD5s and IPs are lower on the Pyramid of Pain because they are quick to change. Therefore, looking into the future, a threat analyst should be working up the pyramid to prevent future attacks. As we have learned previously, it takes more work for an attacker to alter TTPs and tools. It is much more likely their indicators will remain relevant further into the future.

Using indicators for future threat intelligence can certainly be difficult. However, getting in front of the threat is the best way to prevent damage from ever occurring to the environment.

Preventing Damage Versus Certainty

One of the interesting concepts of timing is that the further ahead an analyst looks to predict an attacker's motives and actions, the more difficult it becomes. The increased amount of time allows attackers the ability to change their tactics, but the analyst's ability to mitigate damage also increases. When looking into past incidents, it is better to use lower-ranked indicators because of their ease in gathering. Implementing changes for future attacks is difficult; it is much better to be following because information tends to remain static when looking into the future.

Assessing Risk

Entire courses have been designed to determine the best way of assessing risk. One of the goals of an effective threat-intelligence program is to help determine the likelihood and cost of events impacting the organization. Entire books and certifications have been developed to help identify and measure risks in multiple fields, so I will concentrate on simple guidelines to remember when determining your own risk metrics.

Beware Unquantifiable Feelings

There are many summaries of the human condition and how we try to assign risk. Whether we do this consciously or unconsciously, risk is determined more through a feeling than through metrics. Unfortunately, these funny feelings are perhaps the most utilized method for determining risk at a company. However, information gleaned from this method is not transparent, can vary widely based on people's perceptions, and cannot be duplicated. Unless your company makes major decisions based on bad feelings alone, it should be clear that numbers are needed to justify a threat posed to a company.

Creating a Risk Calculator

A risk calculator is a useful, quantifiable measure to determine how risky the threat is to an organization. The security community already tries to use this method when looking at vulnerabilities. The CVSS score, developed in 2004 by the National Infrastructure Advisory Council (NIAC), is used by a great number of people when trying to describe just how bad a system vulnerability is. While this method is still qualitative, it provides transparency, clearly defines requirements, and allows senior management to make changes and corrections in a processed manner. However, the CVSS score does not take into account threat actors; rather, it just looks at the environment. Therefore, I propose to use a similar model looking *only* at the threats.

The end state of the calculator is to provide a quantitative value to a threat actor. Similar to the CVSS rating's range from 1 to 10, a higher score denotes a more robust threat actor. People can easily understand that a high threat is worse than a low threat, and this method allows analysts to provide their managers a quantified score. Over time, a chart of different threats can be developed to help track how threats present risk to the company.

Threat Versus Vulnerability

I break the chart into two scores: the outside “Threat” and the company “Vulnerability.” I prefer to do it this way because

- A threat does not control the business operations or dependencies. Businesses decide which patches to update, how much to spend on defenses, and whether to update software and what vulnerability to accept.
- A threat actor will shift to different vulnerabilities. Compartmentalizing the vulnerability allows the reuse of the threat score as the threat actor shifts to a different vulnerability. Conversely, a vulnerability score can also be used for many different threat actors.

It is easier to change the vulnerability than the threat. As you will see, a business is rarely going to be able to alter the attributes of threat actors to make them less dangerous. However, the vulnerability can be mitigated in several ways.

To understand vulnerabilities, I would suggest following the CVSS rules. They are readily used throughout the industry already. However, there is not a complementary method for developing a threat score.

Quantifying the Threat

My approach to a threat model is similar to CVSS. I compare a variety of qualitative attributes to come up with a quantitative score. This is not something new or difficult. If you were to discuss the risk of baseball players getting on base, you could look at several attributes that can be linked to their skill. Have they been playing long? Do they play baseball professionally? Do they have time to train? It is easy to ask these simple questions and then rank several baseball players without even seeing them play. We will do the same thing for threat actors. Personally, I like to split a threat into two major categories, persona and targeting.

Persona (Who Are We Dealing With?)

Persona is the person or the group that is doing the dirty work forming the threat. Some popular threats in the news are the named threat actors like "Berserk Bear" and "APT-3," which are organized groups of professional criminals. Less-defined groups such as "Anonymous" and "Lizard Squad" are good examples of hacktivists. It would be rather safe to say that nation-state actors are more advanced and more dangerous than hacktivists. What we need to do as threat analysts is determine why this statement is true.

Persona	1	2	3	4	5
Experience	Very little experience, has not coordinated a campaign	Little experience, can discover vulnerabilities	Some experience, can discover unique vulnerabilities	Experienced, capable of writing zero days to achieve objectives	Very experienced, has conducted multiple campaigns
Personnel	Fewer than 5 hobbyists	Fewer than 5 employed	5+ employed	10+ employed	40+ employed
Resources	No funding; less than $1,000	Some basic funding; less than $10,000	Small enterprise funding; less than $1 million	Professional company; $1–10 million	Nation-state funding; $10+ million
Tools	Utilizing only a few publicly available tools	Widely used, publicly available toolsets	Designs custom tools and purchases specific toolsets	Designs custom tools and purchases specific nonpublic toolsets	Creates or purchases private zero days, malware, and toolsets
Determination	Fearful of attribution and will call off attack if spooked	Will delay attack if there is interaction with their victims	Willing to steal and defraud victim	Willing to interact with victims to steal money and commit fraud	Do not believe they will be caught or don't care if they are

Management and other analysts should not have to take one analyst's evaluation at face value and should have methods to double-check their work in a quantified manner. More importantly, as more threats emerge, we need a method to convey how certain personas are more advanced than others. This allows helpful conversations regarding the threats and, more importantly, a discussion on how to take the appropriate actions against them.

I have come up with a few ideas regarding their ability or attributes for your consideration. I like to consider this a spectrum: the personas will improve and degrade over time but should remain relatively stable. Significant events can impact these threat actors, and their scores can change, sometimes rapidly. Extended training, recruiting new consultants, recent arrest of key members, seizure of infrastructure, and so on are all indicators that a persona's capability may have rapidly changed. The lone wolf who just got placed in prison is certainly much less of a threat after he or she is behind bars.

Targeting (Who Are They Going After?)

Threat intelligence is concerned with the bad guys' motivations and choice of targets. Targeting is simply assessing what objects the attacker is looking for. Some common items are credentials, personal bank accounts, and research data. If we know a company has this type of data, we know it is more likely that the attacker will be targeting the company. Bank robbers don't go to bakeries; they go to banks.

Knowing we are being targeted allows us to change the posture of the company in order to help prevent damage. However, it takes time and resources to always be vigilant, and so it is important to raise our shield only when absolutely necessary. Being able to understand this concept is an important aspect of threat intelligence.

A more targeted attack will take actions specific to the attacker's intended target. This increases the risk to the company, as the more time attackers spend understanding the environment, the more likely they will be successful at breaching the victim's defenses.

Imagine an e-mail campaign sending out spam for "Long-lost aunt; huge inheritance." How much effort should be used protecting the environment from this threat? I would suggest not much. Historically, these types of e-mails were sent out to many people hoping for at least one click.

Now imagine a meticulously crafted company memo with official letterhead and matching logos sent to a select few individuals. This targeted attack takes more time, but it is more likely to evade spam filters, and employees are more likely to follow the request. The second example is much more dangerous. These two different levels of targeting show a much different risk to the company.

Now that we have established the importance of understanding the adversary's targets, how do we measure it? As an outsider, there are several difficulties. Primarily, it is rare that threat actors will preemptively call out their targets. There is a large tactical advantage for threat actors to hide their intentions and their targets. (However, a good counterexample is hacktivists or groups who blackmail companies and explicitly state their targets to instill fear.) A concealed attack is much more effective when the targeted individuals are unaware they are under attack, and any exploits will have a greater chance of success.

Unfortunately, determining if your group is being targeted is often reactive. To make the difficult step into being proactive, the best hope is finding out that other groups are being targeted and act from there. A carmaker might look at other car companies; a bank should look at other banks, and so on. Understanding what is happening at other organizations is the best way to determine what will soon be happening to yours.

Exploit Life Cycle

A unique bit of insight to preempt threat attacks is to compare where an exploit is in its life cycle. Exploits tend to follow a similar development trend:

1. The exploit concept is discovered.
2. An exploit is demonstrated or exploit code becomes available.
3. The exploit is actively used outside of a test environment.
4. A patch is released.
5. Use of the exploit declines as the vulnerability is patched.
6. All systems that can be patched are patched.
7. Unpatched systems are slowly replaced by new software and hardware that are already patched.
8. As systems are discontinued, the exploit use continues to decline.

9. Exploit code still remains but at much less risk.

While this is all interesting, as threat analysts, we are most concerned with the first four steps. It might seem callous, but a threat analyst should not be concerned if the rest of the world is patching an exploit or if the exploit falls into disuse. An analyst should be concerned about whether the exploit is being used and the impact to the business if the vulnerable systems are not patched. With this insight we can go into using the information from the exploit life cycle to suggest proactive remediations.

Bringing It Together

To create a simple targeting model, I combine the exploit and targeting scales. Therefore, I propose the following values for targeting.

Targeting Values

1. No concept exists: There are no indications that a vulnerability exists. I debated even including this category, but I think it is useful as a means to create a placeholder for a piece of key infrastructure.
2. Concept exists: A vulnerability, CVE, or alert is out for a vulnerability that has not been demonstrated by security experts or attackers to be reliable.

3. Exploit is demonstrated: The attack concept has been demonstrated, and modules from toolsets exist. Some examples include code released on GitHub, a metasploit module, or a walkthrough of the exploit online.
4. Targets of opportunity: The exploit or malware has been used against an organization—perhaps a spam campaign with malicious links or a web-vulnerability scan across the Internet.
5. Targeting a culture/region/language: A country, region, or cultural subset that is similar to yours has seen this exploit. Sometimes campaigns are contained to a specific region. A popular virus discussed by Symantec targets Japanese banks. It takes additional resources to ensure the language is correct and convincingly meets cultural norms.
6. Targeting peers: The exploit is being used to target individuals you would consider peers. Several researchers group peers by North American Industry Classification System codes (education, manufacturing, accommodation, defense), but I suggest leaving the definition of "peers" up to your organization. Some additional suggestions might be

the energy industry, government entities, nongovernmental organizations, and journalists.

7. Your company/clients: You see examples of this in your company, using websites with similar templates to your websites and/or with your clients. An unexpected e-mail from john@yourcompany.com certainly should raise the level of awareness in your company.

Determining a Threat Score

By combining both the persona and targeting scores, an overall score is created for the threat actor against your company. How you combine the persona and targeting scores is a matter of personal preference. Here are some ideas:

1. Add the persona and targeting scores together.

   Persona is 5
   Targeting is 4
   Overall (5 + 4) is 9

2. Create a table to compare the two traits.

Persona is 6
Targeting is 5
Overall is 4

		Targeting						
		1	**2**	**3**	**4**	**5**	**6**	**7**
Persona	**1**	N/A	1	2	3	4	5	6
	2	N/A	1	2	3	4	5	6
	3	N/A	1	2	3	4	5	6
	4	N/A	1	2	3	4	5	6
	5	N/A	1	2	3	4	5	6
	6	N/A	1	2	3	4	5	7
	7	N/A	2	3	4	5	6	8
	8	N/A	3	4	5	6	7	9
	9	N/A	4	5	6	7	8	10
	10	N/A	5	6	7	8	9	10

3. Create some funky math. Take the sum of the numerator divided by the denominator. I multiply mine by 10 to make it easier to compare with a CVSS score

Persona is 5 of 10
Targeting is 4 of 7
Overall (9 of 17) is $9/17 \times 10 = 5.3$

Different methods will produce more usable information depending on the organization. I would encourage playing around to see what works best for yours.

Using CVSS Score with Threat Score

I have found that the CVSS score fits in nicely with the threat score. After all, an organization needs to determine the presence of a threat, a vulnerability, and a business impact for that threat. By using these elements to create a business case, we can highlight additional needs for infrastructure, additional personnel, or, most likely, an expedited patching process.

Similar to combining scores of persona and threat, the CVSS score can be combined to create an overall risk. Part of the reason I like to keep my threat score out of 10 is so that it matches up with the 10-point scale of the CVSS score. This makes math really easy to get an average.

Here are some more examples of how to add scores.

1. Add CVSS and threat-actor score together.

   CVSS is 6
   Threat is 4
   Overall (6 + 4) is 10

2. Take an average

   CVSS is 6
   Threat is 4
   Overall (10 of 20) is 5

3. Multiply and then divide by 10

   CVSS is 6
   Threat is 4
   Overall ($6 \times 4/10$) is 2.4

Each method produces quite different responses. The importance of this exercise is making sure these numbers are valuable to the organization. Personally, I prefer to make the score out of 10 because it is demonstrable, repeatable, and consistent with other expectations.

Putting the Numbers into Action

To help understand some of these ideas of determining and using a threat score, we will walk through some examples. A new vulnerability is published called "foul pig." The vulnerability has the following characteristics:

- Impacts Tomcat servers
- Remotely executable
- Easily gains remote access and persistence. Greatly impacts confidentiality, integrity, and availability.

The threat actor is a highly experienced, well-funded, and well-trained criminal organization. However, it is targeting a different business sector within your geographic area. While currently an exploit exists, it hasn't been observed targeting organizations.

What would you rate this threat as?

Correlating and Storing Threat Information

Some consideration needs to go into how all this threat information is stored. With all the information that is being processed, it is important to get it to all the team members who are using threat intelligence in their day-to-day business. There are several methods that groups use or default to in order to share intelligence.

No Storage Program in Place

The most likely scenario is for an organization to not store intelligence data. Instead of taking the time to process and document data, they simply hold it in personal accounts. This is the default situation where nothing is stored in a centralized location for the threat analyst, engineers, executives, or security personnel. It remains the default because it costs nothing and requires no infrastructure or investment. Perhaps the information is all kept in a folder in their e-mail box, or it stays in a web portal where they received it. These methods provide a place to hold the data, but they do not help the dissemination of information to other people.

The major concern is that this method creates a point of failure dependent on the analyst. If the analyst is out sick or leaves the company, all the threat intelligence for that analyst is unavailable. Also, depending on the size of the threat-intel feeds, analysts might be overwhelmed by the many services, and the information could be difficult to sort. Although this is the default process, having no storage creates a difficult situation where a company is heavily dependent on the analyst.

Unique and Proprietary Services

Some companies use unique web applications/portals to store their threat information and share it throughout an organization. This is an improvement over no storage because it allows information to be shared with other people at the organization. However, it is still difficult to integrate with a threat program, because often the service is not built for additional information that analysts will likely want to store.

A common complaint with this method is that valuable insight and coordination among different threats are not being carried over to other defenders. An additional concern is that the amount of information may overwhelm the service and could be difficult to sort through.

Databases

Companies are continuing to build larger databases to warehouse data. These services can be a fertile ground for correlating threat intelligence. Not only can these services hold large amounts of information, they can also be changed so that they can correlate the data among threats.

This can be helpful for analysts especially when they are dealing with a large number of indicators from threat actors. This is especially true with technical indicators (MD5s and IPs) where the databases would be able to link some indicators together. Databases are made just for this purpose, and there are additional utilities that make sorting threat intelligence easier and more readily accessible.

The weakness of just setting up a large database is developing the interface for communicating these findings to responders and stakeholders. Even the best-correlated information is useless until this happens.

Proprietary Portals

Some threat-intelligence vendors provide a proprietary portal that holds all the threat-intelligence data the vendor is sharing. The professionalism of these sites can vary considerably, from simple portals showing text files to fully interactive sites and APIs integrating information directly into your environment. While a threat analyst will not be able to add proprietary information into the portal, the web portal may allow the company to meet its objectives of providing information to all the required persons.

The quality of the portal depends on each vendor. Sometimes these portals provide adequate information to meet the needs of the company. However, if an analyst discovers something new to add, it is a cumbersome process to add this information into the portal. The inability to add information to a threat repository can be a large concern if a company is using multiple proprietary feeds.

A proprietary portal can be an efficient way to provide large amounts of data; however, the value of the information to a threat-intelligence program will vary considerably. If the information cannot be acted upon or does not concern your company, it is more noisy than valuable.

Threat-Information Repositories

A threat-information repository approaches what might be the highest standard for a storage method. Designed specifically to hold, correlate, and distribute threat information, repositories allow a threat analyst to easily input information and share it among team members.

All repositories utilize a database to help store, parse, and disseminate threat intelligence. Unlike traditional databases, a threat-information repository is uniquely designed with presets for threat information, allowing an analyst to easily input and communicate relevant threat information. Using a database's correlation capability and indexing allows the repositories to quickly discover trends within the information that is stored. It then provides a method to communicate this information back out to the community. These prebuilt configurations reduce the need to hire developers to create custom solutions.

Another advantage found with a threat repository is the ability to share information among multiple groups, even some outside the company. By rapidly communicating back and forth with various stakeholders and allies, information can be shared as it develops. To reach this end, many repositories are exploring protocols such as TAXII, STIX, and CybOX to help share the information in a coordinated fashion.

The drawbacks of threat-information repositories include the amount of effort and cost associated with setting them up. They are not cheap. Additionally, communicating threat information is a touchy subject, and setting up valuable peer relationships with companies you trust can be a difficult task. With information being shared almost instantaneously, you would not want to send or receive the wrong pieces.

Choosing What Fits Your Model

How a threat program stores information is important, and the most expensive option might not provide an accompanying level of value for the company. If the threat-intelligence program has only a limited number of analysts, it might be best to work with just a proprietary solution that closely matches the company's profile. If the analysts expect to be doing lots of attribution through malware review, the ability to correlate information across a team might justify more robust solutions.

Additional Considerations

At this point, I would expect many experts to start discussing how there are many other factors to decide whether a threat is actually dangerous to your company. This is certainly true, and there are some additional considerations a threat analyst should look at when developing a threat-intelligence model.

Models Are Not Perfect

One of my favorite quotes regarding model creation comes from George Box, who states, "All models are wrong, the scientist cannot obtain a 'correct' one by excessive elaboration…Just as the ability to devise simple but evocative models is the signature of the great scientist so over elaboration and over parameterization is often the mark of mediocrity."

Or, as I say, "Keep it simple."

Spending countless hours designing the perfect model to account for every eventuality is difficult. More importantly, an overly complex model might not help produce a usable solution and might make the problem more difficult. The relatively simple model I have provided can quickly be built, described, and used by any threat-intel analyst.

Quantifying How Much Risk Is Reduced

When deciding which safeguards should be put in place, it is useful to determine how it will impact the overall information-technology environment. It is even better when a threat analyst can give a quantitative number on how much risk is reduced.

Creating threat ratings with proposed controls will give you numbers to compare with the baseline. The difference between these numbers will allow a quantified improvement to be estimated. By examining several risk ratings, you can determine the best course of action.

For example, the threat actor "Alice" targets web applications. We have determined that Alice's threat score is 5. In the current unpatched environment, the CVSS score for a new vulnerability is 7.

Control A reduces the CVSS score to 5.

Control B reduces the CVSS score to 1.

We can see that both of the controls reduce the overall risk score and by how much. Of course, the decision among doing nothing or using control A or control B has costs associated with it. If you have numbers beside dollar signs, a better risk discussion can take place for mitigations.

Another example is this. The new threat actor Bob's threat score is 9, and the same CVSS scores are used.

The magnitude of the differences in the first example is smaller than in the second. I use this to point out that the severity of the threat score drastically impacts the overall risk score. The numbers also suggest that if a more dangerous threat actor is directly targeting the company, vulnerability mitigations will have a greater impact.

Weighting of Values

Weighting information is a method to add emphasis to the numbers representing areas of the business. Certain threats or vulnerabilities might be weighted more heavily if they show an exaggerated risk to the company. While it is important to weigh information, make sure this is done in a consistent manner. On several occasions I have seen threat analysts weigh information to provide the data they want to meet an agenda. People tend to cherry-pick information to suit their needs and are more than happy to change a model to justify their beliefs. This was discussed in the metrics section, but it does bear repeating. Don't be a jerk and use numbers to justify your own agenda.

Dynamic Changes

It is important to note that these ratings will change and can change rapidly. "Shellshock" and "Heartbleed" have taught us that exploits can lie dormant for years. An exploit that has not yet been developed and then suddenly emerges targeting various industries will have its risk rating changed several times. The sudden emergence of an easily adaptable exploit calls for additional diligence for reviewing and possibly increasing the risk level.

The Scaling Problem

The danger of a threat is rarely a linear function. Similar to hurricanes and earthquakes, the strength of a class 1 is orders of magnitudes lower than that of a class 3. Similarly, the danger a threat forms against a company can go from very low to very high in an expedited manner.

Clustering

One of the items noticed is that when scoring various metrics, events tend to cluster in some models. CVSS does this often. Either an event is low, medium, or really high. There is not really a middle ground for vulnerabilities.

While this might seem like a small issue, it does present some difficulties. As items start to cluster more and more, it is difficult to determine which threats are more dangerous than their peers. If all the threat actors are being grouped at 7, how do we choose which one to mitigate? To prevent clustering, more information on threat actors can help lead to more granular models and spread out the clusters.

On the other hand, clustering might not be a problem for your organization. If there is enough information to act on, additional granularity might not be beneficial or lead to more-informed decisions. Maybe you can easily mitigate a large number of 7s quickly. In this case, it wouldn't matter if one were ranked higher than the other—only that they were completed.

Recency or Boy Cried Wolf

If your company has just burned the midnight oil chasing a vulnerability, another threat will likely be met with less exuberance, if at all. Human capital and goodwill are incredibly important and difficult to come by in an organization. If it is all wasted for a response that is unwarranted, it can be demoralizing for the team and the business.

A possible solution is making sure the team has some recoup time. If you just pulled people from their anniversary dinner or their kid's soccer practice, you had better make it up to them! It will be much cheaper than trying to find a replacement.

Bayesian Algorithms and Machine Learning

There are many discussions surrounding the use of Bayesian algorithms and machine learning to determine a threat over time. I am very interested in exploring these methods and possibly putting out the equations for them in the future. While my current method only has snapshots in time, trending based on historical data is certainly the next step toward better understanding and automating threat-intelligence metrics.

Collaboration and Growing of Threat Intelligence

Collaborating is fantastic among members of communities. The overlap of targeting can be a great indicator of how threats are targeting different members and evolving. However, some companies may value different indicators differently. Threat analysts will need to make a decision about how closely they should be receiving feeds from different threat-information–sharing communities.

For example, the Carbanak group has typically targeted banks and is best seen through financial transactions. If the information sharing centers on malware targeting tellers, a company that is not a bank would not gain as much from these indicators.

Another example includes the recent popularity of point-of-sale (POS) malware. If your company uses POS systems, this information is useful. However, if your group doesn't use POS, then it isn't useful information. I can't mark off when the information is going to meet the threshold of being useful intelligence; however, there are certainly collaboration groups that will distract more than help the program.

Implementing Threat Intelligence

Implementing threat intelligence requires a number of important factors to consider. The environment needs to be understood so that the intelligence is useful. Tactical intelligence allows an analyst to stop an imminent threat but lasts momentarily. Strategic intelligence will take more work to implement but provides more robust protection. Some indicators will be more useful for the situations in your environment. Qualitative and quantitative metrics each should be used to ensure that threats are defined and properly communicated. Threat intelligence is like a garden: an analyst cannot just put it in and forget it exists. It requires constant maintenance to be effective. Correlation and storage will take time, but the best solution will be up to your analysts.

Summary

1. What does your environment look like?
2. What are the key pieces of information your company will need to make a decision?
3. What are some alerts that would be beneficial for your company?
4. What are the difficulties involved with hunting external threat actors versus internal threat actors?
5. What are some devices that can add threat intelligence into your environment?
6. Describe the types of threat actors that would target your company.
7. What is the difference between tactical and strategic intelligence?
8. List three quantitative and three qualitative metrics.
9. Why is it easier to look for past threat indicators?
10. What is the relationship between the certainty of intelligence and usefulness of that intelligence?
11. When investing in a threat-intelligence program, what can be one of the lowest-cost solutions?

12. What is a CVSS score, and how is it related to threat information?

13. What are some indicators that would suggest your company is being targeted?

14. What is the general tendency of threats as they move from the bottom of the Pyramid of Pain to the top?

15. Why are repositories a valuable tool for anyone analyzing threat intelligence?

Questions for Consideration

You have just joined a smaller entrepreneurial outfit created by one of your friends. The business is rather simple and does editing for several small publishing firms. They upload their copy, editors make changes, and they send the edits back to the author.

1. What are some key pieces of information you will need to protect?
2. What kinds of alerts will help you determine if your company is under attack?
3. What types of threat actors would likely target your company? How would you know the company was being targeted?

You work for a small Internet café. It has computers and work space for customers who are trying to get additional work done on a high-speed connection away from home. Customers are given a small slip of paper with a code on it to receive Internet time at the counter, or they can insert credit-card details when logging on to the Wi-Fi.

1. What are some threats to your computers? Who would the threat actor be?

2. What metric could you gather to see if employees are giving away too many codes?
3. What is the lowest-cost solution you could use to help protect employees? How about customers?
4. What types of threat feeds should you get?

3

Building Your Threat-Intel Program

In the military, our intelligence teams are amazing. We have so many smart and dedicated personnel in intelligence that the intelligence communities have splintered into their own subspecialties. Military watch floors act as a centralized location to take in and push out information to many unique and complex operations. These military centers are so successful that their operating model has been adopted by businesses. More recently the business operations centers have consolidated into what is commonly called a security operations center (SOC). In this context, a SOC is a centralized location to manage various aspects of IT security and will be one of the largest consumers of threat intelligence.

A SOC's size and specialties depend on the needs of the company. Large companies will employ a different makeup of individuals than smaller ones. In fact, if you look at the SOC as the hub for all information related to a particular subject, a smaller company might just have a single person functioning as their SOC.

Threat-Intelligence Maturity Models

Consider the size of your threat-intelligence program. Hopefully, you have a rough idea of the intelligence you are looking for and what will create the biggest impact for your company at the lowest cost. When looking at the maturity of a company's threat-intelligence program, I have noticed around five different levels in which threat intelligence is gathered. By considering the varying levels of maturity, companies can ensure their programs fit their unique needs.

Level 1: No Plan—IT Professionals

The most basic type of threat program is the absence of any plan. Threat intelligence is not explicitly planned for, and any information gathered is done in an ad hoc manner. No employees are tasked with looking at threat intelligence. There are no procedures, no understanding about what important information is needed, and no guidance on what information should be collected to make decisions.

This is the default situation, and it can happen in companies of all sizes. Some companies might not even be aware of some of the dangers across the world. Since no information is gathered or used to make decisions, the company is not aware of new threat actors, their techniques, or how a breach might occur. There are no additional costs associated with this type of setup, but there is a large amount of risk.

Level 2: No Plan—Moderately Experienced IT Professionals/Dedicated Responder

To take a step in the right direction, model number two uses moderately experienced IT professionals. While they continue to conduct their day-to-day operations, they also dabble with security and threat intelligence in some shape or form. Perhaps they understand the basics of cross-site scripting or wireless attacks. However, there is still no greater planning or training program to decide if there is adequate security to protect the company against the current threats.

Exposure to new techniques and mitigations of threat actors can allow the security team to react to alerts and understand what they are seeing. Perhaps abnormal behavior will trigger an admin to go back and look at information or cause technicians to isolate a computer. In both cases, the goal is to let the analysts understand the different ways in which a current adversary will act in the company's environment.

Level 2 models can be cheaply obtained by having security personnel take training courses detailing current attack methods and casually monitoring open-source threat information. Understanding basic indicators and impacts in the current threat landscape will help the IT professional recognize and correctly identify a problem if one occurs. Fortunately, many companies can easily reach this level.

Level 3: Simple Plan—Moderately Experienced IT Professionals/Responders

At level 3, the program starts to identify key components of the company, and the threat analyst is looking to better maintain and update information about the adversary. The key components and critical assets of a company are unique and require some effort to understand. Understanding the unique nature of the environment requires a custom solution and research into the company's operations. Only then will an analyst be able to prioritize which bits and pieces of information should be acted on in the environment. Knowing the critical points of infrastructure helps better target essential systems. A responder with this knowledge can concentrate on information relating to these key elements.

It is important to note that there needs to be a plan of how intelligence is used before you move forward. If there is no plan to develop information into threat intelligence, the company is not making anything safer and is spending effort to build a beautiful but useless report.

Level 4: Developed Plan—Dedicated Intelligence Position

A dedicated analyst position is the next big investment a company can make. Not all companies will need to reach this level. Perhaps responders are able to take care of most of the threat intelligence while completing their daily routine. Maybe the threat can be mitigated to such a narrow scope that the additional employees are not needed. A dedicated intelligence analyst uniquely ensures that there is enough time to work on developing a more robust plan. By creating workflows, determining critical points of infrastructure, monitoring decisions, and measuring the effectiveness of mitigations, the team is able to reduce risk from threat actors.

If indications are similar across multiple areas, threat-intelligence analysts can be a force multiplier. Quickly, they can determine if other people are observing a discovered indicator. This allows them to pass this information forward to the rest of the team, saving the responders valuable time.

While tactical intelligence is vital, the biggest value a threat analyst can provide is to help shape overall security and strategically protect identified assets from threat actors.

Think of it as figuring out how to apply an ounce of protection to prevent a ton of pain. It is possible to meet these goals without an analyst, but the solution is more robust when a dedicated analyst is able to pursue strategic objectives.

Level 5: Developed Plan—
Dedicated Intelligence Team

An entire dedicated intelligence team depends on having an extremely robust response team. As a force multiplier, it only makes sense to have a dedicated team if there is an excessively large amount of information that needs to be sorted through. Even the largest Information Sharing and Analysis Centers (ISACs) only have a couple people sorting threat intelligence. However, if it is needed, the larger team also allows for a much higher throughput, which can be helpful when looking at large amounts of information.

As the size of the team grows, a large emphasis should be placed on the ability of analysts to share information throughout the organization. Different groups and sections of the company may request different information from the team regarding threats, and being able to educate them is a unique advantage that a threat-intelligence team can provide.

The problem is that this larger team can be very expensive, and it might be hard to justify the size of a large team. As with all large teams, processes need to be on point; otherwise, inefficiencies will drive everything down. Therefore, special caution should be considered when hiring a large team, as continuous feedback needs to be given back to the business.

Maturity Models Wrap-Up

The best way for me to summarize is with a quick PowerPoint image. As you become more mature, you get more security personnel and develop a better plan. Not every organization will need a dedicated intelligence team. Many will do fine with just a simple plan.

Lvl	Plan	Personnel	Added Spending	Additional Benefit
1	No plan	IT professionals		
2	No plan	Dedicated security		
3	Simple plan	Experienced security		
4	Better plan	Dedicated intel analyst		
5	Amazing plan	Dedicated intel team		

I would also like to draw attention to how the amount of spending increases rapidly, while the additional benefit of more threat spending diminishes. For markets with large amounts of money to protect them, it probably makes sense to reach these high levels. However, in cost-constrained groups, reaching the higher levels might not be cost-effective, and that's okay.

How Many People Should Be in a Team?

The maturity model I present only suggests the size of a SOC (responders, intel, operations, etc.). This is intentional, as the number of analysts required will largely vary from company to company. Some considerations when determining size are these:

- Number of employees and business processes at the company. The more employees and processes in the company, the larger the attack surface and more potential threat actors targeting the company.
- Number of threat actors. Take quick stock of the number of bad guys you believe are threats to the company. Each additional threat actor will require additional research, correlation, and data storage. To help reduce this load, more threat analysts will need to be hired.
- On-call hours. If you are running a 24/7 watch floor, you will need at least five dedicated analysts so someone is always pulling a shift. Six if you want any of them to ever have vacation time, training, or the possibility of being sick.

- The variety of critical data and rapidly shifting architecture. The more diverse the data, the more time the analysts will need to spend understanding what they are trying to defend and the unique challenges of each one.

At the end of the day, it is really about the amount of data the analysts will be sorting through. If there is an enormous amount of data, and your analyst is getting buried, then you might need to get another.

Is that answer too vague? Need a cheat sheet? Start with at least one analyst per thirty IT personnel, and scale up as needed from there. It's a great rule of thumb.

Too Many Intelligence Analysts

One potential problem you could face is having too many threat-intel analysts for the amount of work you are doing. If that is the case, they can be used to go over past information and update old intelligence. After all, intelligence changes rather quickly.

During slow times it is also a great opportunity to use intel analysts as responders to understand processes, concerns, and procedures. The cross-training helps them understand what is needed to remediate incidents. Another option is to have them work in other areas of the business. Analysts shadowing their business counterparts can teach about other jobs, IT concerns, and risks. In either case, the analysts are learning valuable skills to help them produce good information.

Intelligence Does Not Have to Come Just from Dedicated Analysts

All IT personnel are doing some level of threat intelligence. They might not have all the fancy feeds and repositories of a SOC, but they can still understand the basic indicators, TTPs, and emerging threats just by being in the profession. A dedicated threat analyst is ideal, but don't be blind to the great resources all around you. Having a few intelligence enthusiasts might be everything you need. Make sure you can find a way to include their input to the team.

Properly Leveraging Human Capital

Running an intelligence program can be very time-consuming. With so many subtle thoughts and messages, it can be easy to get lost between what is good and what is bad. It is such an epic task that I have seen managers spend months looking for the right analyst.

When looking across your company, remember the following concept: Everyone is an intelligence analyst. From your top executives to your newest line workers, they all bring in bits and pieces of understanding to the environment. Being able to leverage everyone at the company and leveraging their expertise creates great benefits for the organization.

Look for Hidden Talent

Most security personnel know a few things about threat intelligence. Perhaps they just know the preferred tactic of an adversary from years ago. That tidbit of information is still useful to help push out important knowledge. It could be the driving force for creating segmentation in an otherwise flat network or removing dangerous programs that make employees vulnerable.

People are the best sensors. They are much more in tune to the importance of what is going on in an environment. If they find a compelling new story about threat actors, they are likely to tell other people about it. As a threat analyst, you need to make sure they also tell you. They should feel empowered to submit information to the intelligence team. Not only will you gain quick insight into current events, you will also know what people are interested in at your company. I often see compelling stories from other people who saw something on the news or "know a guy" and bring me interesting information before it comes out in more formal channels.

Not Overdrawing Your Human Capital

Burnout is common among highly trained professionals. Good staff members complete more work than most of their peers combined. The problem is how their success causes more work to be added to their queue. In essence, businesses love to burn out their best employees. When managing a threat-intelligence group, you have to be cognizant of what your morale is. A dip in morale can rip apart compliance on procedures and may lead to an exodus of your best people for greener pastures.

I had the pleasure to work with SEALs during my time in the navy, and it was certainly the most enjoyable job I have ever experienced in my career. Like InfoSec personnel, SEALs are highly trained individuals, which you always need more of. Despite long hours, dangerous situations, and high demands, they rarely burn out. While this work response is in a large part due to the type of people they are, an even bigger factor is the culture they cultivate.

Culture of Technical Excellence

Everyone is expected to be excellent. Instead of lecturing on excellence, demonstrate it every day. Strive to be an expert in both your job and your lateral duties. This includes realizing that some other employees might be better than you at some things. When you recognize this, you should learn from them. Short presentations or talks that allow experts to feel good about what they know are a great confidence boost.

Allow your employees some time to pursue and grow unique ideas to help the company. Although it might not be on the path you have developed, the sense of autonomy provides a tool for employees to feel like more than just cogs. The importance is not how the project helps the company as much as how the project will help the employees better connect with the company success. I have been surprised at how frequently efforts like these have provided a measurable business benefit, while building up a culture in which people are excited to excel.

Transparent and Unbiased Results

When something happens, good or bad, ensure that information is relayed to the group. Information travels quickly, and attempts to hide it never work. Normally this just obscures the good and highlights the bad.

When we achieve a goal, receive feedback, or have some criticism, I ensure that it is quickly provided to the group. This rapid feedback replaces rumors and speculations with information employees can act on. Problems can be solved, good work can be duplicated, and employees are not left trying to figure out what might be going on. It is not healthy for information to stagnate for months when it could be in production the next day.

Recognition

One of the quickest ways to build rapport with employees and managers is to promptly and publicly acknowledge the efforts of everyone on a successful project. Nobody thinks you have completed a major project yourself, and not providing credit to employees can be viewed as dishonest. There is no need for you to take credit for your work; by your discussing it, everyone knows you are involved. However, if you omit someone's contribution, that person will remember it forever and be less likely to assist in the future. If employees are working on a project together, they need to follow these guidelines as well. By providing credit, you let contributors know you value them and their work as employees. Properly credited, they are more likely to work together well in the future.

These are not new ideas. In fact, they are already pushed throughout management literature. However, threat analysts are typically very unique in the difficulty to find and replace them. Creating a culture that respects and properly manages highly trained individuals is essential to have a successful threat-intelligence program.

Team Tasking

As organizations get larger, people naturally separate off into different responsibilities. At some point an effort to formalize processes should occur to help describe objectives of the individuals and ensure that work does not overlap.

I have seen teams built in many ways, and they tend to be a combination of the following. Depending on your situation, there are different methods for getting threat intel into the group.

No Separation

I have seen models in which there is no separation across the organization. Everyone on the team is a jack-of-all-trades, and the team works together to get the job done.

A potential problem is that people don't specialize enough in a needed area. Analysts can get bogged down in one instance and never move on to something else that is more important. Since no overall tasking is occurring, many things can be dropped through negligence or believing another team member has the tasks. Redundant work is also a concern, since multiple people could be working on the same threat information. Managing all these tasks become a colossal job and can create some problems.

This is a typical configuration for a very small team or if the network team is an army of one.

How intel is ingested: Intelligence is gathered in a very informal manner. There is little to no oversight or prevention of overlap.

How you can drive improvement: Create a small mechanism to bring together threat information. Have a small meeting to bring different groups together to discuss recent discoveries, thoughts, and ideas. Provide a place for everyone on the team to share information they feel is important and relevant.

By Device

Sometimes a group is the expert on a given piece of technology (firewalls, proxy, antivirus). They might be in charge of maintenance, updates, and all aspects of the devices associated with it. Therefore, it just comes naturally for them to run the intelligence associated with the devices as it falls into their day-to-day operations.

One concern with this approach is that the device owners are policing themselves. There is a large disincentive in searching out and looking for flaws in their products. It is much easier to turn a blind eye toward things if they feel it is in their best interest to do so. People are overly interested in their own products. Some bias about the importance of their products can bleed through into their risk calculations.

This is a classic tactical approach, as everything is being done at the device level. Depending on the size of the team, there might be some great benefits from device-less employee provide strategic oversight on how everything is running.

How intel is ingested: Teams tend to get information from the vendors of their product or from open-source technical forums. Since this flavor of intel is highly technical, it often does not apply much outside of the immediate group.

How you can drive improvement: Ensure that the different device teams are working together so that gaps are not created among the different groups. Consider appointing someone over the flow of information across the teams.

By Process/Function

A much more refined method is separating out tasking by function. Perhaps you have small groups of people working from initial planning to decommission a single section of the business. Maybe one team handles web, another the network, and another the e-mail. The separation allows for clear swim lanes and responsibilities. Devices with similar functions might be grouped together, such as firewalls and web proxies. It is good to have somebody who understands what can and can't be done on these devices and presents these limitations to the group.

A problem with this method is that the context of a threat might be lost. Someone just looking at DDoS traffic might not understand that the actual problem was a misconfigured web scan. Additionally, the groups can play hot potato with difficult problems and simply push the blame from one team to the next. This uses up valuable time while not solving the issue.

Assigning responsibilities by process is a popular method if the accountability of the security team is not done in a centralized manner. It can be much easier to simply split teams along those same lines. The analysts can concentrate on exactly what their seniors are interested in.

How intel is ingested: Information is typically gathered through relation to the function. If an analyst is in charge of a specific application, he or she will continue to receive information regarding the application. Similar to the device method, there are major concerns about gaps, which could exist between processes and in informal processes.

How you can drive improvement: If separated into groups, be sure to have some exercises where the groups coordinate with other functions. Some type of centralized authority is almost required to help prevent groups from ignoring or playing hot potato with issues. Without sufficient exercises, a lack of communication could be a problem.

By Time

Having run a 24/7 watch floor, I have learned lots of little tricks and techniques over the years.

The first is understanding where information is coming from and the providers' operating hours. Staffing toward the times of high volume should seem obvious, but sometimes it is ignored. If information comes in at a trickle at night, the nighttime staffing requirement should be less. If it only comes in from Sunday to Thursday, staffing should reflect that.

The biggest challenge with having a 24/7 watch floor is the overhead from transferring information at shift changes. Great effort goes into ensuring that no information is lost or misinterpreted when transferring between shifts. I have seen these transfers create large amounts of work and lost productivity in organizations as small and large details are accidentally omitted. It can be so disruptive that hours of work can be lost to simply ensure everything is set up correctly. To help minimize this risk and work, it is best to design a schedule having fewer shifts and a workable communication plan.

How intel is ingested: By the time a 24/7 analyst floor is created, it is likely they are drawing information from multiple feeds. However, a large component of time is spent communicating information over a shift change. This provides a handoff point for the oncoming team.

How you can drive improvement: Breaking up analyst duties into concrete and easily defined sections is another beneficial technique. As one part is finished, it can be easily picked up by the next analyst. I like to imagine this process as building tiny modular containers. As the containers are completed, everyone knows what to do with the container. Confusion is mitigated, so the next analysts don't have to be caught up and can jump right into the work.

Perhaps an analyst putting the information into the repository is one discrete step. Another step might be taking information and putting it into the networking remediations. Another would be putting the information into the e-mail remediations. By having small, concrete steps, pass down is streamlined.

Ensure that tasking is broken into smaller portions, allowing analysts to finish sections and easily hand off the data to the next analyst.

By Geography

For very large companies, there is also separation by geographic location. Having groups in different areas can dovetail nicely into the time model. It can be great for one team to be finishing up in London while another starts in New Zealand.

Having local analysts who understand both the culture and the environment is also essential to getting work done in different areas. Some places act differently than other locations. The local focus can allow intelligence that is specific to the region.

Separating a team by geography offers many of the same challenges as separating by time. There is a higher emphasis on properly communicating information and handling findings. Regulations in different regions can also impact information gathering, storage, and correlation of logs and private information. Having local experts in these regions is certainly a helpful tool to ensure that the company plays by the rules. Despite some of the difficulties in communication, a company with a global presence should seriously consider having regional experts.

How intel is ingested: Similar to the time-segregated model, geographic models share the same concerns of shifting data. However, a unique cultural perspective might be beneficial when operating in a region. Local intelligence feeds might be present that relate to the business there. Alternatively, some threat actors only operate in specific cultures to conduct social-engineering attacks.

How you can drive improvement: Simply having small groups of analysts in a region can help provide a unique viewpoint of threat actors, challenges, and important projects in the region. By pushing regional experts for unique insights at their location, an analyst will be able to determine if different methods are needed.

The Rock-Star Paradox

One problem occurs when you start seeing the creation of rock stars in an organization. There is always at least one person who seems to be better than everyone else on the job. The rock star is the analyst whom other people run to whenever they have an additional problem or concern. Although it sounds like a good goal to develop a rock star who is skilled at everything, this person will become the chokepoint for getting work done. If more and more people and processes come to rely on this person, it creates a self-feeding loop. The rock star will get more and more responsibility without offloading anything to other team members. Success for a rock star is being rewarded with even more work.

The difficulty of a rock star is twofold. Other team members will become apathetic, will not be as involved, and may not understand how they are able to contribute. A drive for perfection might lead to the transfer of work from an analyst who is not doing a "perfect" job to the rock star, diminishing the other analyst's opportunities to learn.

With additional loads and responsibilities, the rock star will put the organization in a difficult place if he or she is absent. Projects might not be completed as groups wait for the rock star's input. Also, organizations will need to be careful not to burn out the rock star. If this person takes leave or finds another job, the company is going to be at a huge disadvantage until the rest of the team catches up.

How intel is ingested: The rock star is already getting all of the intelligence; however, he or she will not have the time to process or document it. It is rarely communicated out to the teams.

How you can drive improvement: If you see a rock star starting to develop, make sure to properly manage the amount of additional responsibilities going to that person. Use the rock star as a mentor to teach other team members and transfer tasks. Lean heavily on other analysts to learn from the rock star.

Do not let a rock star's plate overfill. Ensure that the rock star takes vacation, trains others to replace him or her, and is not working in excess. If the standard is not set early, you are greatly increasing the risk of not catching the problem until it is monstrous.

The best way to use the rock star is for the most difficult projects that only that person will be able to do. The book *The Phoenix Project* is a great example of how the reliance on one person was horrible for an organization and the problems with developing a rock star.

The Importance of Rotating Analysts

Rotating analysts to different time, device, or function groups helps them build experience and a wide range of understanding. Getting fresh eyes on a project to see issues can also help take care of difficult problems in innovative ways. The greater understanding can help with communication among groups and coordination of effort across functions, devices, or geography.

Be Careful about Crying Wolf

Now that we have built a robust process to help detect and react to threat intelligence, we might have created a new problem. There is always an example of something being broken and exploited. Constant reporting like this can create a narrative in which nothing is safe, everything will be breached quickly, and the world is doomed.

This is dangerous!

No executive will want to constantly hear that the sky is falling and the world is ending. This persistent overreaction can create learned helplessness in those who constantly hear it. Excessively pushing this narrative can create an environment where executives start believing there is nothing they can do to make the environment safer. Even worse, executives won't act because they perceive that nothing can be done.

There is an interesting human dynamic where the only thing worse than being wrong is being the only one who was wrong. This is even truer in high-stakes environments where decisions can cost jobs. It is easy to save face if you fail while following best practices. But if you fail while doing something unique, people tend to be very critical. This creates some initial inertia for making changes in any environment.

There is a simple solution. Before bringing threat information to executives, ensure that the message you bring to them has merit, a solution is measurable, and you even have some examples of other people doing something similar. This might take some time, but following these steps helps make their decision easier and your recommendations more palatable.

Building a Constructive Narrative

When communicating with other stakeholders, the first thing you should find out is their concerns. Excited energy is good, but energy not directed at the problem can derail your progress. Truly knowing their perspective builds rapport and helps build an understanding of what is expected from the security team.

Aggressively pursuing measures not in line with stakeholders' expectations will create more tension among the teams. An intelligence analyst might appear out of touch and seem to be suggesting methods that waste the company's money or hinder production.

Therefore, I suggest reaching out to stakeholders well ahead of time with a few questions, such as these:

- What IT security news has been most influential in changing your operations this year?
- What are your three biggest concerns?
- When should your team be informed about security concerns?
- Is there someone on your team I can work with before escalating to you?

- I think you might be interested in *X*, because it directly impacts your *Y*. Would that be helpful?

Then just listen to the responses. Without burying the company with terror stories, an analyst can provide valuable threat intelligence to help protect the company. Delivering properly scoped and escalated information will help reassure them that the information is relevant and properly weighted.

How Much Does It Cost?

The truth is "it depends." I have provided several examples that range from using an IT employee with open feeds for free up to building an entire team. However, there are a few areas where I think you can get some great bang for your buck and others where you get less of a payoff.

Better Training Equals Better Employees

Training is by far the cheapest way to improve your ability to process threat information into threat intelligence. But before comparing the costs of technical classes, certifications, and trips around the world, consider some even easier and cheaper methods.

Instead of going out and trying to find that rock star able to do everything, attempt to build expertise in-house.

Growing the capabilities of current employees is almost always cheaper.

Having one-hour training sessions taught by an employee is also an efficient method. It provides a way for analysts to understand a topic better, train other employees, and show off. It is also one way to make your overall group, SOC, or company more threat savvy. The costs of this are minimal; at the worst, the team will have attended a meeting that was a waste of time. But how many times have you sat through a useless meeting?

Normally I would caution against letting individuals choose their own training experience. Individuals may gravitate toward choosing areas of interest unrelated to their main job functions. Although it is true that analysts should concentrate on something that is similar to their current environment, some lateral thinking is not a bad prospect. This is especially true if your employees show interest in the training. Additionally, it can be used as leverage to get training that an analyst is interested in combined with information that he or she is not yet pursuing.

Try training anyone who shows interest in advancing or taking more responsibility. Training courses can be an ego booster, and valued workers can be properly trained to fill in gaps of the threat-intelligence team.

Hire Great Employees

Hiring IT professionals is difficult. Finding someone with an intelligence background and IT background is even harder. An impressive résumé full of education and training does not make a good intel analyst. An analyst also needs the social skills to work across several groups and coordinate with many different technologies. Additionally, a good analyst will meet the needs of many other jobs in the marketplace. The combined requirement of education and social skills with the high demand for competing resources creates an environment where finding a person fitting all of these skills is like finding a unicorn. The hiring manager's job will be hindered by the ability to recruit from a tiny group of talented individuals.

Altogether, this makes hiring intelligence professionals expensive. However, people meeting these requirements can bring in unique resources as well. With their personal connections and resources, experienced analysts can find the latest news and discover problems for unique situations. This added networking can often be a great resource for a company to have at their disposal. Reaching out to solve problems is difficult, and having friends to help when the going gets tough is beneficial.

The Benefits of Certifications

Training courses may seem expensive, but they are still much less expensive than equipment, feeds, and outsourcing intelligence work. For the price of a single intelligence feed, you can almost always get at least twenty-five courses of expensive education.

Certifications help give merit to the team being well trained. Although certifications are not a perfect standard and many contain gaps of understanding, they do help provide a basic framework to show understanding about their subject matter.

Also consider your current technology vendors. Almost all service agreements encourage you to reach out to the vendor to receive additional training. The training can be free of charge and can help make the team run more effectively with what you are already paying for. Firewalls, scanning tools, and so on are all trying to help the company detect the bad guys. Additional training detailing what to look for and other best practices can help turn more threat information into good threat intelligence.

Training is a more expensive method to improve threat-intelligence capability. Realistically, it is cheaper than some alternative methods. Also ask company security vendors if they can provide training for products to make the technologies used by analysts more effective.

Cost of Threat-Intelligence Feeds

Threat-intelligence feeds can be an expensive way to augment a threat-intelligence program. Having a high number of indicators, feeds are designed to quickly be added into an environment.

To help make the feeds more specific to a company, most vendors state that their feeds are tailored. I normally see tailored intelligence feeds with granularity only down to the industry they serve. This is not a bad thing; as I covered in previous chapters, it is important to consider what threats are targeting similar companies. However, an analyst needs to carefully consider whether such feeds are meeting the specific needs of the company. Since the feeds are put together by another company and sold to other customers, it is unlikely they will be tailored to meet the exact needs of an analyst. Like all other sources, threat-intelligence feeds need to be vetted to determine if they meet the needs of the company.

Cost of Outsourcing to Vendors

If you don't want to develop a threat-intelligence program, you can always buy it for a price. Plenty of companies out there will be willing to build you an "intelligence in a box" solution for threat-intelligence needs. But it will cost you.

Besides monetary concerns, there always needs to be consideration of how close the program is aligning to organizational goals. A company might not be concerned with phishing, but the monitoring solution provided by the vendor could monitor phishing exclusively. These points of friction can be difficult to reconcile after a contract is signed.

If you are outsourcing, it is important to make sure the vendors are quantifying their work. Be active and look at some of the measures discussed regarding the quantity and quality of the vendor's metrics. If they produce good ratings, make sure they explain why. Proactive involvement requires understanding, and it won't happen if you don't ask questions.

Getting a vendor to take care of a threat-intelligence gap can be expensive. Ensure that they are documenting their work and quantifying their results. Otherwise, I suggest shopping elsewhere when the contract expires.

Threat Intelligence Supporting Network Security

One of the biggest successes for threat intelligence is how it is able to support network security. I have thoroughly discussed how indicators can be used to help defenders find new leads when looking at logs and alerts. These roles are so interconnected that in stages two and three of the threat-intelligence maturity model, defenders will be the employees responsible for conducting threat intelligence. This makes sense, as analysts are looking at logs, seeing what is anomalous, and making a decision to remediate or ignore the anomalies found. This is also why several of the maturity models I propose do not include a threat analyst until later stages. An informal method, with informal analysts, might be exactly what the company needs.

When alerts are seen throughout the environment, it is a good practice to involve the threat-intelligence team. A dedicated threat analyst will have a larger strategic picture of where the indicators fit in, and other relations could be formed. By definition, a dedicated threat analyst will be able to process more information and, with the help of a good repository, provide valuable insight to responders as events are investigated. By making good decisions about which events to escalate, threat intelligence can accelerate investigations of anomalous events and incidents.

Pentesting and War-Game Support

I have conducted pentests for some time, and they are always lots of fun. It is great to pretend being bad—to swing around the big club and see what breaks. However, being the big bad wolf is rarely useful without some context.

Intelligence-driven penetration testing is more effective for two reasons:

1. It better represents the threat a company faces.
2. An analyst has evidence that these types of events take place.

I remember one test I was on where we took control of the entire system. My team spent many hours working late, bent over backward to meet scheduling, and faced an on-site IT group that was hostile toward our efforts. After we wrote our report, it was beautiful, dense, and heavy. We showed time and time again how we were able to get to the core systems vital to network operations. With grins on our faces, we waited around for a response.

One month passed…

Two months passed…

Three months passed…

After the four months, we received feedback. We were told our findings were wrong. Flabbergasted, I read one comment: "Unrealistic test. Capability not demonstrated by the enemy."

This sent me into a rage, because they were able to dismiss our findings with a single line, and my team's hard work was tossed out. Therefore, I started including threat intelligence in every test. I used the exact same tools,

CVEs, and indicators I found in intelligence reports on all my tests.

It is important to be able to give additional threat context. To say we used tools consistent with a threat actor, exploited the same CVEs seen by past breaches, and had a substantial impact that mirrored a real-world example is a very powerful narrative. Executives are able to see themselves in these situations. Threat intelligence makes it more real, and the context from intelligence is helpful in showing why things should be fixed.

The Cyber Kill Chain: Working through a Process

The cyber kill chain is an interesting model that helps explain an attack. It borrows most of its elements from the targeting kill chain used in the planning sessions of US military operations. The concept of the kill-chain details the steps needed for a group (friend or foe) to conduct a successful attack. The cyber kill chain is similar, and by understanding these phases, defenders are better positioned to stop an attack. However, there is some confusion on the chain that needs to be clarified.

Broken down into its elements, the cyber kill chain consists of:

1. Reconnaissance
2. Weaponization
3. Delivery
4. Exploitation
5. Installation
6. Command and control (C2)
7. Action of objectives

Each of these steps can take from several seconds to several months. Threat intelligence gathered by an analyst can concentrate on distinct actions that threat actors take during each of these stages.

A useful aspect of the kill chain is that a responder can mitigate an attack and move on quickly. If the kill chain is already broken in one place, breaking it in four other places is not essential. By definition, stopping one step will break the chain and stop the forward momentum of the attack. This allows a team to reassess the risk and move on to the next biggest threat. If used in this manner, a kill chain can be a great way to decide what actions need to be taken. In particular, gathering threat information can lead to decisions on chokepoints or stages to gather additional information.

Looking at the cyber kill chain can be the ideal starting point for responders, as it can provide a method to step through an attack that has already happened. Knowing there are command and control (C2) elements of malware provides a mechanism that can be detected, discovered, and stopped. In essence, a defender can look at different steps and walk back through to discover the installation of software, how the exploitation occurred, how it was delivered, and so on.

Preemptively breaking the chain is more difficult. The intent is if the chain is broken at any link, the attack will not be able to continue, and the attack is prevented. It logically follows that all subsequent links are dependent on the first, and an early success will prevent a successful attack. A shortcoming of this model is that attacks are less like a chain and more like a mesh.

When penetration testing, we had multiple methods of reconnaissance and multiple weaponized payloads to use, and we could deliver them instantly. During reconnaissance I might find five or ten different exploits for a particular vulnerability, each one with a weaponized payload ready to be delivered. Attackers are able to build on thousands of "chains" and easily discard the ones that don't work or might be prevented.

The kill-chain model was originally developed for the military and relied on the understanding that assets and resources had some physical limitations. There are only so many missiles, drones, and bullets. However, the delivery phase of a phishing campaign is remarkably cheaper than a missile salvo or an airstrike. The disproportion of effort in the most common of scenarios makes the cyber kill chain great for protecting against widespread unskilled and untargeted campaigns but is less useful against attackers exercising a bit of flexibility.

The kill chain also seems to break down with some of the newer threats. Ransomware is ripping through business networks, will conduct little to no reconnaissance, and starts actions on objectives before establishing C2. For example, ransomware depends on the encryption of files, which would qualify as actions of objective (step 7). Blocking C2 (step 6) will not prevent the ransomware from encrypting essential files. A better defense for malware is being able to rapidly recover the data in the event of an attack. While it is not part of the chain, this helps prevent damages from all malware instead of a specific instance. In this case, and in many others, simply planning a successful recovery is more important than trying to block the chain.

Kill chains are great models to help define what threat information is needed to defend against a threat and are helpful for responders as they walk through the steps of an attacker. The kill-chain model can prioritize actions needed to mitigate damage and help push for remediations that need to occur to defend against them. However, preemptive mitigations can be more problematic if trying to stop dedicated threat actors.

Giving Your Team Better Experience

Receiving and acting on intelligence requires some work and experience combined with good sources of information. Experience continues to be the best teacher, but it is also the most elusive. Fortunately, a few places exist where an analyst can get a better idea of how threat intelligence can be used and what tactics the threat actors will be using in the future.

Conferences and Other Gatherings of the Mind

Security conferences and meet ups are quick ways to find people with similar interests in exploring the motives and actions of threat actors. Conferences offer valuable resources and opinions about topics you normally wouldn't experience.

The information-security community has grown greatly, and so many interesting people are exploring new ideas in the field. There are so many solutions, so many new vulnerabilities, and so many new technologies that we can't possibly keep up as individuals. However, as a community, there is a better chance of understanding what is happening and what will be coming in the future.

If we are able to gauge what people are seeing, what they are doing, and what they are valuing when problems occur, we will be able to

- Have colleagues to reach out to when bad things happen, and
- Explore certain attacks before seeing them in the environment.

The prices for attending a security conference can range greatly. The location, venue, speakers, vendor sponsorship, and training provided can all factor into the price. Overall, they are great places to meet people, see what is trending in the community, and learn what might be coming in the future.

Some major conferences to consider are Black Hat and Defcon. Both of these are held during the same week in Las Vegas. I love Defcon because of all the villages, the interesting people, and the insightful talks. Every time I go, I learn at least a dozen new things, break a few toys, and come back happy. However, these both can be rather expensive conferences. Black Hat training can run into the thousands, and it is hard to expense a trip to Las Vegas without the accounting department raising an eyebrow.

Other conferences offer some of the same benefits in a more intimate setting. Shmoocon and Recon are smaller conferences with some very interesting people. Additionally, Derbycon has some fantastic training for some of the cheapest prices I have seen.

Vendor

Vendor conferences are typically free and provide you good food and refreshments, neat swag, and some training from the sponsoring vendor. Offering many of the same perks as other conferences, vendor conferences just require the analyst to acknowledge the bit of salesmanship found in new products.

While it is great to explore for key components in your network technology, it is a bit polarizing. Most of the discussion will point toward the sponsoring product. If you have a hammer, everything looks like a nail, and vendors are selling that hammer. Just make sure not to neglect the rest of your toolkit.

Local Conferences and Meet Ups

The best value for both your time and your budget are local conferences and meetings. With applications like Facebook and Meetup, the ease of coordinating a group is ridiculous. Low cost and low travel time make these a prudent way to get the benefits of a bigger event but fit it into a normal time allocation and budget.

Local conferences have been growing in popularity. B-Sides conferences are amazing, as they offer a small venue where people can gather from the local community. While you might not be able to see some of the big names, you can meet people who live close by and are willing to do projects. In any case, it is an opportunity to grab the beverage of your choice to chat about security.

Hackerspaces are also a quick way to find people and explore different thoughts and ideas. Many are sprouting up across the world, and you can easily perform a Google search for one close to you.

Online

Of course, online there are many resources and groups you can find to discuss a wide range of topics. Daily news sites, message forums, e-mail distributions, and even chat rooms all have ways in which people are passing on information about their projects and passing on what they recently have seen.

Distribution of Data

One interesting dilemma for a threat analyst is how threat intelligence is distributed across an organization. Does it go to everyone? Just a few people? How will it get there? There are now many mechanisms that can be used to move data to different stakeholders, and there are no set rules on what should be done. Most of it will be situational and based off the expertise and desires of your executives, responders, and customers.

Depending on the severity of the intelligence, an analyst might need to confirm receipt of the message. Sometimes an analyst will need a quick back-and-forth of information at a rapid speed. More formal documentation is required if the information is going to be presented to someone at a higher level. With all these challenges and opportunities, here are some considerations for the most common communication methods.

E-mail

E-mail is seen in almost every organization across the world because it can be sent to a wide range of people quickly. However, in a rapidly evolving situation, e-mail is cumbersome and slow. E-mails can become out of sync and splintered into their own independent threads. Therefore, the best use of e-mail involves sending out data that will not be changing, such as reports.

Editable Documents

With online services like Sharepoint and Office 365, documents can be rapidly shared and correlated among multiple parties. It can be a good method for tracking and documenting processes used to watch an evolving threat. While processes can be tracked, sometimes there is confusion if multiple people are editing them at the same time.

PDFs

The preferred method for sharing reports and sending things up to executives are PDFs. They allow graphics, are readable on almost every device, can be locked, and can be watermarked to help protect the documented information. However, they are painfully difficult to change and would not work well while reacting to a situation. They are more suitable for the final report to document everything, once the event is over.

Chat Rooms/Services

Being able to exchange quick bits of information is key during an incident. Private chat rooms are helpful because they keep a log of every message sent, time-stamp the message, and can allow immediate feedback. This is my preferred method of coordination through an incident and for sharing intelligence with responders.

Since writing in a chat room is an informal matter, the scripts and logs would not be sent to executives, as they can be long, tedious, and filled with acronyms and technical jargon. Therefore, they are normally used in conjunction with a follow-on report to clarify major points and incidents during an investigation.

Tracking Services

A tracking service ensures that tasking is automatically assigned to the appropriate people. Ticketing services have been useful for normal trouble tickets, which leads into properly responding to incidents. If intelligence is found in the environment that needs to be acted on, a ticketing service ensures that the tasks required are assigned to the appropriate personnel and tracked until completion. Additionally, it has time stamps and creates a record of tasks that may need to be documented in a future after-action report.

Phone Calls

The real value of phone calls is that you instantly know someone is aware of a situation as you talk. The feedback during a phone call is instantaneous. In all the previous examples, the communication was only one way, like a broadcast. Phone calls allow people distributing the intelligence to ensure that the appropriate party both understands what they are saying and can confirm the actions they are taking.

Phones calls are difficult to track and document. Recording the conversations also seems more inappropriate than in the other forms of communication, and doing so might violate privacy laws. Therefore, they are best used for immediate information passing with a follow-up communication by another method after the situation has been handled.

Conference Calls

Similar to phone calls but with multiple people, conference calls are valuable during an incident because team members can rapidly discuss the situation while injecting threat intelligence and remediations under way. Unlike in chat rooms, it is more difficult to send over information like syncs, technical indicators, and so on.

Videoconference calls add a visual aspect to the conference call. Screen sharing can help show other people what you are doing, and being able to walk through a process can be invaluable when explaining unique indicators or problems.

Like the phone calls, this information is rarely recorded and not easily searchable on follow-up. Therefore, it might be a best practice to setup conference calls and designate someone to take minutes to distribute to attendees.

Texts

Like phone calls, texts can offer an immediate response. However, unlike phone calls, texts can be sent out to multiple people at once. While most people keep their phone on them at all times, they might not have access to it. So while the response might be more rapid than an e-mail, a text is certainly not confirmed as quickly as a phone call.

In Person

Perhaps the best method is the oldest, where analysts and responders are all speaking face-to-face. You know that the person is receiving the information, and you can interact quickly. The biggest problem is that larger companies are geographically diverse, which prevents people from meeting on a daily basis. This is helpful for responding or enacting controls, but this often needs follow-up for what is discussed. Everyone forgets little details and gets pulled in many different directions; therefore, it is best to meet face-to-face for planning and big issues and to remember to follow up with an e-mail.

Distribution Lists

Part of this is my military background, but I feel it is very important to maintain distribution lists for different situations. It is always better to maintain an updated list than to scramble for names at the last second. Having a distribution list for both e-mails and text messages ensures that you can rapidly send out the needed information to exactly the right people.

Keeping the list well-groomed is important. Ensuring that required information only gets to the correct recipients is paramount in streamlining the process, not getting off topic, and rapidly reaching the end result you want.

What Will the Leadership Be Looking For?

When communicating messages, keep things simple and focused on the business impact. If anybody needs more technical details, they will ask. As technology experts, we take pride in our knowledge, and that's good! However, it gets frustrating when you are giving filler that they either already know or are not concerned about. Pick out the better piece of intel from these two examples:

1. Our company has received 495 attacks in Q1 and expects something similar in Q2. Of these attacks, 200 were for IPs in China; 295 were from other areas of the world.
2. Our company has responded to and mitigated 495 attacks in Q1. We have noticed increasing web-based attacks from criminals and will concentrate our efforts there for Q2.

Choice two is often the better answer. It provides quantifiable data, provides a prediction of who the threat actors are and what their motivations are, and lets managers know the team is already proactively mitigating the threat.

Not the Method but the Message

Getting information out to stakeholders can take on many forms. Each medium has distinct advantages, from ensuring rapid communication to broad audiences to receiving instant confirmation about incidents. Carefully considering your options ensures that threat intelligence can be properly distributed for both low- and high-level threats.

Conveying Importance to a Team

Now that we have pretty numbers and pretty sets of data, I would recommend that we stop and consider what we do with this information. Really dig down deep and ask yourself what you would do in a few scenarios and how you would react to the information you gather. Think of this as a mini war game for yourself.

Imagine there is a level-9 CVSS score, but it does not appear to be targeting your company. What does this look like? Whom would you tell?

If this alert came across now, what would cause you to

- Ignore and turn a blind eye?
- Turn away from your current task?
- Cancel an important meeting?

- Fly to an impacted environment?
- Work late or extended hours?
- Cancel your anniversary dinner?
- Come home from a local vacation?
- Come home from overseas?

What would you do with a more dangerous threat? What about a CVSS 10 that is directly targeting your company; how would your answers change?

As a manager, I would look across the board and determine what kinds of events would cause me to ask this of my employees.

Put down the book, get yourself a drink, and ponder this for a few minutes.

What Do You Value as a Manager?

This miniature war game is a great way for you to practice the motions when you are not under pressure. Plus, it is really easy to practice anywhere—on your commute to work, while you run laps, or while you scribble on a notebook at work. Write down an imagined problem and consider what information you would figuratively kill to get, or ponder your courses of action for various threats. Go crazy, because those five minutes of downtime are perfect to get some practice in.

Once you have a few scenarios figured out, make sure you communicate these ideas for feedback. Some people find it helpful to write these scenarios down in a notebook or a text file. Others choose to just keep them floating around in their brain. Just make sure you can take it out, look over it, think on it, and revise it.

Whichever storage method you choose, I suggest you discuss your strategies with others. Explaining things to a coworker, your boss, your spouse, or your roommate usually helps you understand why a course would be best and which information is essential. If your expectations do not jive with your confidant or have gaping flaws, your plan should be revised. It is also a good idea to update these ideas as you start seeing how they are working out.

Running through these scenarios is a valuable tool to understand what processes are really important in a threat-intelligence program. If, during your small simulations and war games, you find processes not performing as you would like or expect, tweak them. If your threat intelligence exists to drive decisions, this small investment of time can greatly enhance both your processes and communication throughout your organization.

Running a Threat-Intelligence Program

Even without massive budgets, businesses can build amazingly efficient threat-intelligence teams. If properly leveraged, the correct number of people can be maintained to support various business sizes. Teams can be distributed in a number of ways to better align themselves with business processes. Stakeholders can be involved to prevent the constant temptation of raising every threat to executives. Businesses can purchase the correct amount of feeds, hardware, and employees to meet their needs, drive innovation, and properly distribute data. All these considerations can be practiced in order to create miniature war games for the company and refine their process. In doing so, amazing teams can be run to meet the exact needs of your company.

Summary

1. What are some of the costs and benefits when achieving a higher maturity model?
2. What are some considerations when deciding how large your threat-intelligence team should be?
3. What are some dangers of constantly reporting that everything is being hacked and breached?
4. What are some ways in which a threat-intelligence team can be tasked? What are the pros and cons for the different models?
5. What are some costs of developing a better threat-intelligence team?
6. How can threat intelligence support detection and response?
7. What are some ways to incorporate threat intelligence into penetration testing and war gaming?
8. Describe some ways to improve the team's threat intelligence.
9. Why is innovation important?
10. What are some methods used to distribute data to stakeholders?

Questions for Consideration

Over the past two years, your company has started upgrading and expanding its online offerings. This has reached the point where the CIO has put you in charge of helping build a threat-intelligence program. Currently there is no formal security team; instead, professionals wear dual hats of maintaining the applications and protecting them from threats. The company operates on a 24/7 basis but is completely based out of one location.

1. What maturity model would you recommend?
2. How should the team be dividing tasking?
3. What training would you recommend?
4. How will you communicate threat-intelligence data to the CIO?

4

Practice Exercises

Scenario #1

You are an employee going to a foreign country on a business trip. Over the next month, you will be negotiating contracts regarding several dealings between your company and a company in a foreign nation. You are traveling with several items including your laptop, a cell phone, an LTE wireless Internet card, and a hard drive that includes your presentations and potential contracts.

You know the local government has been dealing with political activists over the past few months. Government-backed crackdowns have focused on targeting foreign journalists in the area, claiming they are inciting unrest. Additionally, there has been reporting about people stealing electronics and information.

The same corporation you are conducting business with owns your hotel. It has a free-to-join wireless network. Your company does not have a VPN set up to work with your travel laptop.

1. What are your most valuable assets?

2. Who are some threat actors that could target you?
3. What are some ways they could gain this data?
4. What is the impact if they succeed?
5. What are some ways to mitigate this?

Scenario #2

You are part of a small ten-person business that provides software as a service (SaaS) to businesses. The business users log into your web portal to conduct interactions, and the API feeds information to help them make business decisions regarding purchasing the cheapest products available.

Businesses use the information in real time to make immediate decisions. If the service went down, they would stand to lose money, and they would likely look for another provider.

Your business maintains customer and credit-card information for payments. The credit-card system is dated and will need to be updated to meet new regulations for the coming year.

Currently, the software is being hosted in a cloud service offsite. The company admins use single-factor authentication to get onto the site.

1. What are the assets at the company?
2. How can threat actors negatively impact these?
3. What are the next three steps you should monitor for your threat group?
4. How will they likely harm the business?
5. What is the impact if they succeed?

Scenario #3

Your company, Umulot, has done amazingly over the past few years. It has been so successful that it has been able to purchase the competing company, Blonks. The primary product of Umulot is the creation of specialized widgets used in production. These products are uniquely made, and the plans are a closely held company secret.

Blonks made a competing product, which was defective and caused mishaps at the companies they supported. The resulting legal action caused a massive drop in shareholder price. Umulot was able to aggressively buy Blonks to expand their producing locations and distribution centers. The merger will likely cost many jobs among the former Blonks teams.

The merger is due to start soon, and you are in charge of the threat-intelligence program. How would you deal with the following questions?

1. What is your most important priority and first step during the merger?
2. What are the next three steps you should be doing with your company?
3. What are three threat actors who will try to cause harm to the company?
4. How will they try to do it?

Answers

There are no answers here. I know this seems like a letdown, but there are really no right answers. Even if there were, they all can change within a few years, months, or even days. If you would like to send me your solutions to the scenarios, I will be happy to post them and provide feedback.

Please e-mail me at BookSolutions@mindtrinket.com.

Appendix

A: Program Setup

Set up an intelligence program in five minutes with a sheet of paper.

1. What are the biggest three assets your company is trying to protect?
2. Name three groups of people trying to steal them.
3. What three actions would be the most important to stop?
4. Name three pieces of information that you could collect and that would prevent these attacks from happening.
5. Which sources could provide this information?
6. How much do these sources cost, or do you have services?
7. Who will check these sources and for how long?
8. What will you see if you succeed?

B: Program Review

Review your threat-intel program in five minutes with a sheet of paper. You will need the previous sheet completed.

1. Has the direction changed for the company, or are these still the three biggest areas?
2. Have these actors changed since last assessed?
3. Are these actions still the most important?
4. Have the three sources of information provided any intelligence? Or have you used it to make a decision?
5. Rank your three sources by the value added to reaching these decisions. Does anything stand out?
6. Which source do you feel provided the best information?
7. Should someone else check the sources? Should they spend more or less time on the research?
8. Did you see the signs for success you expected? What will you change for the future?

C: Metrics to Consider

Discovery

- Number of actions taken for detected threats
- Amount of training of the detection team
- Number of dropped or late responses
- Time until an incident is discovered
- Goal: 100 percent of attackers are detected and 0 percent are false

Defense

- Number of blocks generated
- Impact of a false positive
- Time spent putting in mitigations
- Amount of malicious activity triggering
- Impact of false positives and mitigation time

Adversary

- Number of bad guys found in the system
- Number of alerts investigated
- Number of incidents
- Number of actions taken to remediate
- Amount of associated bad traffic
- Time in system before remediation
- Few bad guys in the system quickly categorized

Impact

- Amount of lost revenue from attacks
- Amount of lost revenue from mitigation/false positives

D: Glossary

Advanced persistent threat (APT): Threat actors that have the capability and backing to wage an extended campaign against a group.

Attacker: An entity seeking to harm or take advantage of a company's resources.

Attribution: Assigning the specific cause of an incident or investigation to a threat actor, person, or circumstance.

Command and control (C2): The exercise of authority and direction by an individual to accomplish a goal.

Criminal: A person attempting to gain profit by violating laws of a country.

Distributed Denial of Service (DDoS): Rendering services unavailable by creating large amounts of unwanted or illegitimate traffic.

Hacktivist: A political activist that attacks the IT infrastructure of its target to achieve political will.

Incident monitoring: The processes of watching the IT environment to search for irregularities, indicators, and incidents.

Incident response: The decisions and measures taken to contain and mitigate the effects of IT events to prevent further damage and reestablish normality in the environment.

Indicator: A trend or fact that suggests an event has occurred. Often used to denote similar patterns of threat-actor attacks.

Indicator of compromise: A trend or fact that suggests company data has been or is in the process of being compromised.

Intelligence: Information that is used to make a decision.

Information Sharing and Analysis Center: A nonprofit organization that gathers information on cyber threats to critical infrastructure.

Personal data: Data relating to an individual who is or can be identified either from the data or from the data in conjunction with other information that is in, or is likely to come into, the possession of the data controller.

Phishing: The use of e-mails to attempt stealing, coercing, or tricking the recipient into being infected with malware or to give up personal data.

Proprietary data: Data generated by a company that should be maintained and controlled by the company to maintain competitiveness in the industry.

Rock star: One person in the company who does exceptional work, who is good at everything, and whom everyone goes to for additional tasks.

Signature: A distinguishing aspect, mark, or feature associated with an indicator.

Security Operations Center (SOC) A centralized location to manage various aspects of IT security.

Spear Phishing: A phishing email specifically targeting key employees in an organization.

Threat Intelligence: Information about adversaries that is used to make a decision.

Trusted Automated eXchange of Indicator Information (TAXII): Developed by MITRE, a method that allows for the classification and sharing of indicators amongst different groups.

Threat: An entity which is a source of danger to a company.

Threat Information: Information that helps describes a particular threat. Threat information may be turned into threat intelligence through careful analysis.

Tactics, Techniques, and Procedures (TTP): Outlined in Joint Publication 1-02, TTPs are the art, skill, and detailed steps used to perform a specific task.

References

What is threat intelligence?

"Cyber Kill Chain," Lockheed Martin, last accessed June 1, 2016, http://cyber.lockheedmartin.com/cyber-kill-chain-lockheed-martin-poster.

"Wanted: A Definition of "Intelligence", last accessed June 1, 2016, https://www.cia.gov/library/center-for-the-study-of-intelligence/csi-publications/csi-studies/studies/vol46no3/article02.html.

James Stone, *Information Theory: A Tutorial Introduction*, Sebtel Press, 2016.

"Dark winter," last accessed June 1, 2016, http://www.upmchealthsecurity.org/our-work/events/2001_dark-winter/Dark%20Winter%20Script.pdf.

"Manned Gaming and Simulation Relating To Terrorism and Weapons of Mass Destruction," last accessed June 1, 2016, http://fas.org/irp/agency/dod/dtra/manned.pdf.

Dave Lavinsky, *Pareto Principle*, Na 20, 2014, http://www.forbes.com/sites/davelavinsky/2014/01/20/pareto-principle-how-to-use-it-to-dramatically-grow-your-business/.

"MS SQL WORM IS DESTROYING INTERNET," last accessed June 1, 2016, http://seclists.org/bugtraq/2003/Jan/221.

"Welcome to YARA's documentation," accessed June 1, 2016, http://yara.readthedocs.io/en/latest/index.html.

Nate Silver. *The Signal and the Noise: Why so Many Predictions Fail--but Some Don't*. New York: Penguin, 2012. Print.

Jeffrey Friedman, *Assessing Uncertainty in Intelligence*, accessed June 1, 2016, http://www.hks.harvard.edu/fs/rzeckhau/Assessing%20Uncertainty%20in%20Intelligence.pdf.

Rokach, Lior, and Oded Maimon. *Data Mining with Decision Trees: Theory and Applications*. World Scientific Publishing Company, 2008.

"INTellingence: Open Source Intelligence," Last accessed June 1, 2016, https://www.cia.gov/news-information/featured-story-archive/2010-featured-story-archive/open-source-intelligence.html.

"Heartbleed Bug," last accessed June 1, 2016, http://heartbleed.com/.

Gene Kim, Kevin Behr, George Spafford, *The Phoenix Project: A Novel About IT, DevOps, and Helping Your Business Win*, IT Revolution Press, 2013.

Steve Gold, "APTs: not as advanced as you might think," *SC Magazine*, accessed June 1, 2016, http://www.scmagazineuk.com/apts-not-as-advanced-as-you-might-think/article/345953/

Implementing it

Jaakko Rautanen, "How to Draw Clear L3 Logical Network Diagrams," *Packet Pushers*, accessed June 1, 2016, http://packetpushers.net/how-to-draw-clear-l3-logical-network-diagrams/.

"How Big of a Problem is Employee Theft and Fraud?" accessed June 1, 2016, http://www.incorp.com/employee-theft-and-fraud-part1.aspx.

"How hunt teams can unmask hidden attackers," Hewlett Packard, accessed June 1, 2016, http://www8.hp.com/h30458/us/en/discover-performance/c/enterprise-security/innovation/how-hunt-teams-can-unmask-hidden-attackers.html.

"Pyramid of Pain," accessed June 1, 2016, http://detect-respond.blogspot.com/2013/03/the-pyramid-of-pain.html.

"Advanced cyber threat actors are penetrating networks," Secure Works, accessed June 1, 2016, http://www.secureworks.com/cyber-threat-intelligence/advanced-threat-services/targeted-threat-hunting/.
Tom Gjelten, "Cybersecurity Firms Ditch Defense, Learn To Hunt," *NPR*, accessed June 1, 2016, http://www.npr.org/2012/05/10/152374358/cybersecurity-firms-ditch-defense-learn-to-hunt.

Anthony Di Bello, "Threat Hunting is Not a Hobby – Do It Right or Go Home," *BrightTalk*, accessed June 1, 2016, https://www.brighttalk.com/webcast/7451/111953.

Roderic Broadhurst, "Organizations and Cyber crime: An Analysis of the Nature of Groups engaged in Cyber Crime," International Journal of Cyber Criminology, accessed June 11, 2016, http://www.cybercrimejournal.com/broadhurstetalijcc2014vol8issue1.pdf.

Vashisth, A., and A. Kumar. "Corporate Espionage: The Insider Threat". Business Information Review 30.2 (2013): 83-90.

"Russian hackers breached Dow Jones for trading tips: Bloomberg," *Reuters*, accessed June 1, 2016, http://www.reuters.com/article/2015/10/17/us-dowjones-dataprotection-idUSKCN0SA2IS20151017.

David Talbot, "Cyber-Espionage Nightmare," MIT Technology Review, accessed June 1, 2016, http://www.technologyreview.com/featuredstory/538201/cyber-espionage-nightmare/.

"Targeted Threat Intelligence," Secure Works, accessed June 1, 2016, http://www.secureworks.com/cyber-threat-intelligence/advanced-persistent-threat/understand-the-threat/.

Darin Swan, "Advanced Persistent Threats (APT): Analysis of Actors' Motivations and Organizational Responses to Mitigate Risk," Academia, accessed June 1, 2016, http://www.academia.edu/1803679/Advanced_Persistent_Threats_APT_Analysis_of_Actors_Motivations_and_Organizational_Responses_to_Mitigate_Risk.

"JP 3-13 Information Operations," accessed June 1, 2016, http://www.dtic.mil/doctrine/new_pubs/jp3_13.pdf.

Gordis, Leon. Epidemiology. Philadelphia: Elsevier/Saunders, 2009.

"NVD Common Vulnerability Scoring System Support v2," Department of Homeland Security, accessed June 1, 2016, https://nvd.nist.gov/cvss.cfm.

Dimitar Kostadinov, "The Cyber Exploitation Life Cycle," accessed June 1, 2016, http://resources.infosecinstitute.com/the-cyber-exploitation-life-cycle/.

Gelman, A.; Carlin, J.; Stern, H.; and Rubin, D. Bayesian Data Analysis. Boca Raton, FL: Chapman & Hall, 1995.

Running it

Giora Engel, "Deconstructing The Cyber Kill Chain," Dark Reading, accessed June 1, 2016, http://www.darkreading.com/attacks-breaches/deconstructing-the-cyber-kill-chain/a/d-id/1317542.

The Phoenix Project: A Novel About IT, DevOps, and Helping Your Business Win by Gene Kim, Kevin Behr, George Spafford, IT Revolution Press, 2013.

About the Author

James Dietle is a computer enthusiast with 10 years of experience as a naval officer in the intelligence community and over 13 years of IT management experience.

James started off slinging CAT5, coax and silver satin in exchange for ice cream at the age of eight. During his time at the United States Naval Academy he majored in Computer Science and later received a MS in Computer Information Systems.

As an Information Warfare Officer he has served in Afghanistan, Hawaii, Florida, and Norfolk. During his last tour he led the Navy penetration testing team breaking into ships, submarines, airplanes, and DoD facilities.

While holding numerous degrees and certifications, he feels his best education comes through keyboard mashing, blue smoke from failed experiments, and late night discussions with both veterans and information security professionals.

If you have enjoyed this book please provide a review on Amazon and reach out to James at:

Twitter	@JamesDietle
Linkedin	linkedin.com/in/jamesdietle
Email	jdietle@mindtrinket.com

CPSIA information can be obtained
at www.ICGtesting.com
Printed in the USA
LVHW081124160722
723668LV00026B/974